*Murakami Haruki on Film* offers a timely look at the cinematic adaptations of Japanese writer Murakami Haruki's fiction over the past forty years. Films based on Murakami's work (including *Tony Takitani* (2004), *Norwegian Wood* (2010), *Burning* (2018), *Drive My Car* (2022), and many more) manifest a contradictory impulse to faithfully capture the author's literary worlds while expanding and developing these worlds at the same time. Created by directors from Japan, South Korea, Vietnam, Mexico, and the United States, among other national traditions, these films demonstrate the way adaptations are fundamentally creative works that say something new about the different cultural contexts in which they appear. Though the creative reworking of Murakami's literary worlds threatens to distance us from the author and his work, however, this book argues that the very process of "translating" Murakami from one medium to another references the theme of transformation that is central to his work.

# MURAKAMI HARUKI ON FILM

# MURAKAMI HARUKI ON FILM

Marc Yamada

Published by the Association for Asian Studies
Asia Shorts, Number 22
www.asianstudies.org

## The Association for Asian Studies (AAS)

Formed in 1941, the Association for Asian Studies (AAS)—the largest society of its kind, with over 6,000 members worldwide—is a scholarly, non-political, non-profit professional association open to all persons interested in Asia. For further information, please visit www.asianstudies.org.

Cover image: Nishijima Hidetoshi and Miura Tōko in *Drive My Car* (*Doraibu mai kā*, 2021). Photo courtesy of Janus Films and Bitters End.

Note: East Asian names appear in their native standard, with surname first.

Library of Congress Cataloging-in-Publication Data

Names: Yamada, Marc, author.
Title: Murakami Haruki on film / Marc Yamada.
Description: Ann Arbor : Association for Asian Studies, 2024. | Series: Asia shorts; number 22 | Includes bibliographical references. | Summary: "Murakami Haruki on Film offers a timely look at the cinematic adaptations of Japanese writer Murakami Haruki's fiction over the past forty years. Films based on Murakami's work (including *Tony Takitani* (2004), *Norwegian Wood* (2010), *Burning* (2018), *Drive My Car* (2022), and many more) manifest a contradictory impulse to faithfully capture the author's literary worlds while expanding and developing these worlds at the same time. Created by directors from Japan, South Korea, Vietnam, Mexico, and the United States, among other national traditions, these films demonstrate the way adaptations are fundamentally creative works that say something new about the different cultural contexts in which they appear. Though the creative reworking of Murakami's literary worlds threatens to distance us from the author and his work, however, this book argues that the very process of "translating" Murakami from one medium to another references the theme of transformation that is central to his work"— Provided by publisher.
Identifiers: LCCN 2024043103 (print) | LCCN 2024043104 (ebook) | ISBN 9781952636530 (paperback) | ISBN 9781952636547 (epub)
Subjects: LCSH: Murakami, Haruki, 1949—Film adaptations. | LCGFT: Literary criticism. | Film criticism.
Classification: LCC PL856.U673 Z924 2024 (print) | LCC PL856.U673 (ebook) | DDC 895.63/5—dc23/eng/20240912
LC record available at https://lccn.loc.gov/2024043103
LC ebook record available at https://lccn.loc.gov/2024043104

## SHORTS

**Series Editor: David Kenley**
Dakota State University

**ASIA SHORTS offers concise, engagingly written titles by highly qualified authors on topics of significance in Asian Studies. Topics are intended to be substantive, generate discussion and debate within the field, and attract interest beyond it.**

The Asia Shorts series complements and leverages the success of the pedagogically-oriented AAS book series, Key Issues in Asian Studies, and is designed to engage broad audiences with up-to-date scholarship on important topics in Asian Studies. Rigorously peer-reviewed, Asia Shorts books provide cutting-edge scholarship and provocative analyses. They are jargon free, accessible, and speak to contemporary issues or larger themes. In so doing, Asia Shorts volumes make an impact on students, fellow scholars, and informed readers beyond academia.

**For further information, visit the AAS website: www.asianstudies.org.**

# ABOUT THE AUTHOR

**MARC YAMADA** is a Professor of Interdisciplinary Humanities at BYU. He received a PhD in Japanese Literature & Culture from UC Berkeley. Marc has published articles and books on modern Japanese literature, film, and manga. His recent books include *Kore-eda Hirokazu: Shared Spaces of Filmmaking* (University of Illinois Press, 2023) and *Locating Heisei in Japanese Fiction and Film: The Historical Imagination of the Lost Decades* (Routledge, 2019).

# CONTENTS

1: The Cinematic Roots of Haruki World / 1

2: Crime on Camera: Screening "The Bakery Attack" / 19

3: Unfaithful Adaptations in *Drive My Car* / 37

4: Merging Matter and Memory in *Norwegian Wood*, *Tony Takitani*, and *Burning* / 55

5: Animating Haruki World: *Blind Willow, Sleeping Woman* / 73

Filmography / 87

Bibliography / 93

Notes / 101

# Acknowledgments

Thanks go to my student assistants, David Walter and Kathryn Blau, for their help in the early stages of researching this book. The comments of two anonymous external reviewers, along with the mediation of series editor David Kenley, helped immensely in focusing the argument of early drafts of the manuscript and preparing it for publication. Thanks also go to Jay Rubin, Rebecca Suter, Jonathan Dil, and Gitte Marianne Hansen for reading and evaluating the manuscript during its preparation and for their kind and generous blurbs for the back cover.

I would also like to acknowledge the generous financial assistance provided by the College of Humanities and the department of Comparative Arts and Letters at BYU that provided me with resources and time to complete research and writing. Finally, I am grateful for the generosity of director Pierre Földes who allowed me a sneak peek of *Blind Willow, Sleeping Woman* before it premiered on the festival circuit.

Note: Chapter Four of this manuscript is derived in part from an article published in the *Journal of Japanese and Korean Cinema*, 16 Mar 2020, copyright Taylor & Francis, available online: https://doi.org/10.1080/17564905.2020.1738050.

# 1

# The Cinematic Roots
# of Haruki World

Films based on the fiction of Japanese writer Murakami Haruki (b. 1949) are having a moment. Ever since Murakami debuted on the literary scene with the novel *Hear the Wind Sing* (*Kaze no uta o kike* [1979]), filmmakers have found inspiration in his work. Beginning with the adaptation of this first novel as the 1982 feature *Hear the Song of the Wind*, by Japanese director Ōmori Kazuki, independent filmmakers around the world have sought to capture the Japanese author's unique vision in visual form. The shorts *Attack on a Bakery* (*Pan'ya shūgeki* [1982])—based on the 1981 short story "The Bakery Attack"—and *A Girl, She Is 100%* (*100% no onna no ko* [1983])—based on "On Meeting the 100% Perfect Woman One Clear April Morning" ("Shigatsu no aru hareta asa ni 100-pāsento no onna no ko ni deau koto ni tsuite" [1981])—were both directed by independent filmmaker Yamakawa Naoto. Murakami's sequel to "The Bakery Attack," "The Second Bakery Attack" ("Pan'ya saishūgeki" [1985]), has been adapted several times in shorts, notably by Mexican director Carlos Cuarón, South Korean director You Sang-Hun, and Polish director Michal Wawrzecki, among others. Eventually, Murakami's work would catch the eye of feature filmmakers as well. Beginning with *Tony Takitani* by Japanese director Ichikawa Jun (b. 1948), based on the 1990 short story "Tonī Takitani"; the 2010 feature of one of Murakami's most popular novels, *Norwegian Wood*, by Vietnamese director Trần Anh Hùng (b. 1962); and *Hanalei Bay* by Japanese director Matsunaga Daishi, based on a 2005 short story "Hanarei bei"; the quality of films based on Murakami's stories has only increased.

However, it has not been until the last few years that features based on Murakami's stories achieved the highest recognition in the film world. *Burning* (2018), by South Korean director Lee Chang-dong (b. 1954), based on Murakami's

"Barn Burning" ("Naya o yaku" [1983]), took home prizes from the Cannes Film Festival, the Asian Film Awards, and the Los Angeles and Toronto Film Critics Associations, ending up on several critics' top-ten lists for 2018. Not to be outdone, Hamaguchi Ryūsuke's 2021 film, *Drive My Car*, based on Murakami's 2013 story "Doraibu mai kā," has gone on to become perhaps the most acclaimed film based on a Murakami story, winning awards at the Cannes Film Festival and the Golden Globes and taking home the highest honor for world cinema, the Academy Award for Best International Film, in 2022.

This book offers a timely look at the cinematic adaptations of Murakami's fiction over the past forty years. Reflecting both the enormous popularity of his work worldwide, as well as the efforts of filmmakers to use his stories to deal with issues close to home, these films manifest a seemingly contradictory impulse to faithfully capture the details and effects of Murakami's literary worlds while also expanding and developing these worlds at the same time. Created by directors from Japan, South Korea, Vietnam, Mexico, and the United States, among other national traditions, adaptations of Murakami's work pay homage to "Haruki World," the universe that is home to the elements of Murakami's writing that reappear in his novels and stories. These include quirky characters with mysterious abilities and unusual names, secret passageways that lead to parallel worlds, strange happenings that are relayed in a magically realist style, allusions to British popular music and American literary works by authors like F. Scott Fitzgerald, and even self-conscious references to Murakami's own persona as a writer and translator through fictional characters who take on these professions in his stories.

At the same time, the differences between Murakami's literature and its cinematic versions foreground how adaptations are fundamentally creative works that say something new about the different historical and cultural contexts in which they appear. Though the creative reworking of Murakami's literary worlds through adaptation seemingly threatens to distance us from Murakami and his work, this book argues that the very process of "translating" Haruki World from one medium to another draws viewers closer to the author by enacting the theme of transformation that is central to his work.

The sheer number of films based on Murakami's works reflects the global popularity of his fiction. This popularity began in Japan after the release of his 1987 coming-of-age bestseller, *Norwegian Wood*, kicking off the "Haruki phenomenon"—a movement that eventually spread to East Asian nations like Taiwan, Hong Kong, and South Korea.[1] Readers around the world relate to the experiences of the protagonist Watanabe Toru, a student at a Tokyo college in the 1960s who is involved in a love triangle with two women: the frank and practical Midori and the ethereal Naoko. Jiwoon Baik argues that Murakami's nostalgic view of the 1960s in *Norwegian Wood* resonates with audiences in East Asia who, in the

1990s and 2000s, were experiencing the "dissolution of their national ideologies at the same time."[2] In particular, Murakami's novels and stories found an audience with South Korea's 386 generation, whose members were born in the 1960s and were known for their political activism in the 1980s.[3] Members of this generation, like Murakami and other baby boomers in Japan, experienced a similar sense of loss after their revolutionary efforts were defeated by the development of an expansive consumer culture. Moving beyond East Asia, Murakami has become a bestseller in Europe and America as well, with novels like *Kafka on the Shore* (*Umibe no Kafuka* [2005]) and *1Q84* (2011), which reached top-ten status on the *New York Times* bestseller list. Yomota Inuhiko describes the way Murakami's fiction speaks to audiences around the world:

> Unlike the work of his Japanese predecessors, such as Jun'ichiro Tanazaki and Yasunari Kawabata, Murakami's works are not being translated and consumed overseas as those of an author who represents Japanese culture. In every society, his works are first accepted as texts that assuage the political disillusionment, romantic impulses, loneliness, and emptiness of readers. Only later do they fully realize that the author was born in Japan and that the books are actually translations. While it is true that Murakami is a Japanese writer who writes in Japanese, the cultural sensibility that he draws on, the music and film that appear in his works, and the urban way of life that he depicts are all of a nature that cannot be attributed to any single place or people, drifting and circulating as they do in this globalized world.[4]

Defining "cosmopolitan" as a sense of "belonging anywhere," Wakatsuki Tomoki places Murakami's fiction within the genre of "world literature," which, she suggests, resists the "traditional boundaries of literature grounded in national cultures."[5] She speculates that the basis of Murakami's popularity as a global writer stems from his crafting "odorless" (*bunkateki mushūsei*) cultural landscapes in his fiction.[6] Lacking geographical affiliation, Murakami's *mukokuseki* (nationless) stories, Wakatsuki continues, provide a sense of cultural neutrality through references to global pop music and brands.

Indeed, the relatability of Murakami's cosmopolitan narratives has enabled their circulation around the world. At the same time, the films that have followed the spread of the Murakami wave have often been dismissed as ancillary to Murakami's literary output. Yomota identifies Murakami as "just a novelist" and an "anonymous movie-goer."[7] Indeed, Murakami was, from a young age, brought up as a reader and writer of literature. He was born to parents who were both teachers of Japanese classics, and he was raised on paperback translations of American novels. Accordingly, critics have argued that Murakami is primarily concerned with literary issues in his work. Narrating his fictional worlds, more often than not, is Murakami's idiosyncratic first-person narrative voice, a perspective that does not translate well to the "showing mode" of film, restricting viewers to characters' inner worlds. Furthermore, the world that this deadpan narrator inhabits takes on magical realist elements that, one could argue, lend themselves more to a literary style than a cinematic one. What is more, the metafictional treatment of storytelling that is so common in Murakami's work seemingly finds more meaningful expression in literature than in film. Indeed, the act of writing and telling stories is a central theme in Murakami's novels, like *The Wind-Up Bird Chronicle* (*Nejimakidori kuronikuru* [1994–1995])—a novel in which Toru Okada's search for his wife's missing cat leads to bizarre experiences with a cast of strange characters as he explores the dark underbelly of Japanese society and history. Characters like Lt. Mamiya, the scarred World War II veteran in *The Wind-Up Bird Chronicle*, pen long letters that provide the story-within-story basis of Murakami's writing.

Notwithstanding the literariness of Murakami's work, however, critics also identify an affinity to other artistic forms in his fiction. Even casual Murakami readers will no doubt recognize the role music plays in his stories—references to popular and classical compositions abound throughout his oeuvre. Aoki Tamotsu describes Murakami as "an intensely aural writer" and suggests that "the key to understanding [his stories] lies in the sounds which the texts reverberate."[8] His protagonists listen to an eclectic array of musical selections, including classical works by Mozart, Wagner, and Puccini; the jazz and blues stylings of Duke Ellington and Ray Charles; and of course, classic rock by the Beatles, the Beach Boys, and the Rolling Stones, among many more. Many of his stories and novels are named after pop songs, including *Norwegian Wood*; *South of the Border, West of the Sun* (*Kokkyō no minami, taiyō no nishi* [1992]); and "Drive My Car." Yet music does not just serve as a cultural reference point in Murakami's fiction; musical rhythm is one the most important features of his prose style, as the author himself explains: "My style boils down to this: First of all, I never put more meaning into a sentence than is necessary. Second, the sentences have to have rhythm. This is something I learned from music, especially jazz."[9]

Yet, just as Murakami's texts reverberate sound, they also project images. Though overshadowed by literary concerns, the workings of cinematic representation are also deeply engrained in Murakami's writing, so much so that the relationship between literary fiction and film for Murakami involves a reciprocal exchange: just as his writing has inspired filmic adaptations, so too have the visual techniques of cinematic representation influenced his literature. Murakami acknowledges the image-based nature of his writing by likening his work as a writer to that of an illusionist.[10] His interest in the visual medium of film and theater during the formative years of his education in grade school and college impacted his career as a writer. Along with American novels, Murakami was obsessed with Hollywood movies as a child.[11] During his youth in the 1950s and 1960s, Murakami's father regularly took him to see American films like *West Side Story* (1961) at theaters in Kobe and Osaka.[12] In an essay titled "In the Darkness of the Theater," which he wrote for the volume *Murakami Haruki: Journey into Movies*, compiled by curators at the Tsubouchi Memorial Theatre Museum at Waseda University in Tokyo, Murakami describes cinema as a sacred space during his childhood:

> Before multiplex theatres, DVDs, video, and Netflix, watching movies was really fun. After all, the only way to watch movies was to go to a theater, so I always went enthusiastically. Even if the movie was boring or stupid, I had already paid the entrance fee and had no choice but to spend two hours in the dark anyway, so I tried my best to get something out of it. And if you really put in the effort, you'll find a good scene, or some interesting dialogue (I don't remember ever leaving the theater partway through a film, though I did fall asleep once in a while).
>
> Those habits from my youth have left me with a bunch of strange, but unexpectedly beneficial memories. The effort to find something special even in seemingly boring things, or maybe especially in boring things, has really come in handy in daily life. I learned a lot of things in the dark of the movie theater, things that proved very useful in writing novels. Praise be to the dark.[13]

The impact film played in the early development of Murakami's artistic imagination could have led to a career in screenwriting and even filmmaking. As an undergraduate at Waseda University in the late 1960s, Murakami majored in theater, participating in a program made famous by luminary dramatist Tsubouchi Shōyō (1859–1935). Yet, because he went to Waseda with the intention of becoming a screenwriter, Murakami rarely went to see plays during his time there, preferring to while away his college years at the movies, steering clear of the student protests that rocked Tokyo universities during the late 1960s.[14] During one tumultuous period when demonstrations shut down Waseda for an extended period of time, Murakami saw more than two hundred works of American, French, and black-and-white Polish cinema, along with Japanese classics by Kurosawa Akira and Naruse Mikio, among others—not unlike celebrated Japanese director Kore-eda Hirokazu (b. 1962), who also spent his time as a literature major at Waseda during the early 1980s watching classic cinema.[15] Spurred by his interest in film, Murakami spent hours reading screenplays in the Tsubouchi Memorial Theatre Museum on the Waseda campus, a practice he suggests that influenced his style as a novelist.[16] He was particularly drawn to the screenplays of Billy Wilder's noir classic *Sunset Boulevard* (1950) and Kurosawa's *Stray Dog* (1949).[17] Inspired by his love of cinema, Murakami wrote a senior thesis titled "The Idea of the Journey in American Films" to graduate in 1975.[18]

Murakami's interest in film informs his early writing, manifesting through a multitude of references to world cinema in his stories. His characters discuss films with one another or spend hours in theaters watching classics. Cinematic allusions, which fill his fictional works, come largely from American and European films from the 1960s, 1970s, and 1980s that he watched as a college student. According to researchers at the Tsubouchi Memorial Theatre Museum, there are over 120 films referenced in Murakami's novels alone, not counting the many cinematic allusions in his short stories and essays.[19] Some of these references include works such as *Bring Me the Head of Alfredo Garcia* (1974) and *Convoy* (1978) by American director Sam Peckinpah, referenced in *Hear the Wind Sing*; *The Alamo* (1960) by John Wayne, referenced in *A Wild Sheep Chase* (*Hitsuji o meguru bōken* [1982]); *The Third Man* (1949) by Carol Reed, referenced in *Hard-Boiled Wonderland and the End of the World* (*Sekai no owari to Hādo-boirudo Wandārando* [1985]); *The Sound of Music* (1965) by Robert Wise and *The Graduate* (1967) by Mike Nichols, both referenced in *Norwegian Wood*; *E.T. the Extra-Terrestrial* (1982) by Steven Spielberg, referenced in *Dance Dance Dance* (*Dansu dansu dansu* [1988]); *Casablanca* (1942) by Michael Curtiz, referenced in *South of the Border, West of the Sun*; *The 400 Blows* (1959) by François Truffaut, referenced in *Kafka on the Shore*; *Alphaville* (1965) by Jean-Luc Godard, referenced in *After Dark* (*Afutā dāku* [2004]); and *The Thomas Crown Affair* (1968) by Norman Jewison, referenced in *1Q84*.[20] Many of these films serve as inspiration for storylines and settings in Murakami's fiction. For example, it is hard not to see a resemblance between the protagonist of *Casablanca* and the first-person narrator of Murakami's novels like *South of the Border, West of the Sun*, which, like Curtiz's film, involves a romance between two star-crossed lovers who meet at a bar.

Yet, in Murakami's work, film goes beyond just serving as a pop culture reference point—it shapes the content and style of his storytelling. Aaron Gerow argues that the experience of reading a Murakami novel is just like watching a movie.[21] Kawasaki Keiya suggests that the many dark places in Murakami's fiction where his protagonists see dreams or enter parallel realities—wells, tunnels, locked rooms, and so forth—are indicative of the dreaming that goes on in the darkened space of the cinema.[22] Often, experiences within the theater, and those outside of it, merge in Murakami's stories. In *Dance Dance Dance*, the narrator catches a glimpse of his former girlfriend, Kiki—who inexplicably disappeared in the prequel, *A Wild Sheep Chase*—as she plays one of the main characters in a film called *Unrequited Love* that he decides to see on an extended business trip in Hokkaido.

This cinematic attention to exteriority provides a central way for Murakami's protagonists, including the narrator of A Wild Sheep Chase (1982), to interact with the world. The image-oriented medium of film fits the mindset of Murakami's characters, who struggle to relate to themselves and others as psychological beings. Though Murakami's early writing is mostly relayed through a first-person perspective, as discussed above, Ozawa argues this subjective viewpoint should not be confused with the I-novel, a Japanese style of writing in which the reader is invited to identify a direct connection between narrator and author.[23] Influenced by the style of American writer Raymond Chandler, Murakami's first-person viewpoint is focused on exterior conditions and phenomena; even people figure as material objects to itemize and count in novels like A Wild Sheep Chase.

This focus on cinematic exteriority is evidenced in Murakami's extensive use of metonyms, a device that characterizes both literary and cinematic forms of representation. Metonyms are words or images closely associated to a thing or concept that then substitute for the thing or concept in a given context. According to Roman Jakobson, founder of the Russian formalist film movement, metonyms are central to the way both literary and cinematic media represent larger themes. Murakami's stories, argues Matthew Strecher, utilize metonyms to represent the process whereby the self understands the unconscious world through connections between it and the conscious one.[24] Referencing French psychoanalyst Jacques Lacan's work on language and the unconscious, Strecher argues that Murakami's protagonists make "metonymical links with the contents of their inner minds in order to draw them out."[25] By placing a "nostalgic object" in the mind of the main character, Strecher continues, Murakami creates a "chain of linguistic connections" between this object and its manifestation in the character's reality.

References to physical objects, such as clothing, in Murakami's 1990 short story "Tony Takitani" for instance, draw the protagonist into a world of memory and emotional association that translates effortlessly into a filmic experience. In "Tony Takitani," the title character marries a woman, nameless in the story, who is obsessed with fashionable apparel, only to lose her to an untimely accident. After her death, he hires an assistant to wear pieces from his wife's wardrobe, attempting to revitalize a connection between his memory of his wife and the physical things she left behind. The focus on the material reality of memory in the story facilitates its adaptation into film. The 2004 feature Tony Takitani by Ichikawa Jun draws attention to the "weight of memory" that burdens Tony after the death of his wife by underscoring the metonymical relationship between clothing and his nostalgia. In describing the shooting of the film, the actor, Ogata Issey, who plays the title character, discusses the way clothing comes to signify Tony's memory of his wife: "The focal point of the story is Tony's wife's clothes—a straightforward superficiality. No sooner does Tony try to put the brakes on his wife's excessive penchant for buying clothes then she dies. This seems to suggest that she has been defining herself entirely in terms of the clothes covering her body externally."[26]

Both the metonymical makeup and the fragmented structure of Murakami's early work, in particular, resemble cinematic montage. Before he began to craft sustained narrative worlds in later fictions, Murakami incorporated a pastiche style of storytelling in his early novellas. When he describes the crafting of these works, he uses cinematic metaphors, suggesting he "shot" each "scene" of his stories separately and "later strung them together" instead of writing them in chronological fashion.[27] This is particularly the case with two early works. "On Seeing the 100% Perfect Girl One Beautiful April Morning" involves a nameless protagonist who believes that a woman he walks past on the streets of Tokyo one morning is a perfect match for him. The story opens with a description that sounds like an establishing shot: "One beautiful April morning, on a narrow side street in Tokyo's fashionable Harajuku neighborhood, I walk past the 100% perfect girl."[28] Eschewing narrative development, the five-page work captures one scene—one moment in time—that seems to linger like a visual image in the narrator's imagination.

Even Murakami's first novella, *Hear the Wind Sing*, presents more like a collection of moments than a unified story. Consisting of forty short sections, the novel loosely references Murakami's experiences growing up in Kobe and attending college in Tokyo during the student movements. Taking place over twenty-one days (August 8 to 28) during the summer of 1970, the novella is narrated by a twenty-one-year-old unnamed student who studies at a college in Tokyo but returns to his hometown during the summer. His best friend, Rat, is a novelist, and he sends the narrator copies of his manuscripts each year for Christmas. Much like the time and location that the novel chronicles—the lethargic early 1970s, the ending of the revolutionary period—the work lacks an overall flow. It instead presents seemingly unrelated scenes from the narrator's daily life, providing a tableau of his summer that year. Such snippets include moments at Jay's Bar, a favorite watering hole for the protagonist; a memory in which he and Rat crash Rat's Fiat into a park wall; a flashback to a session with a child psychologist; and a scene in which he wakes up in the home of a girl whose name he cannot recall.

The cinematic imagination of Murakami's fiction developed even more as his writing began to engage themes central to filmic representation: perspective and the narrative gaze. Murakami's experimentation with a third-person perspective in novels and stories in the late 1990s and 2000s reflects a growing interest in the implications of seeing and being seen. In particular, his writing considers the control narrators exercise over those they observe, an issue that is central to the understanding of the gaze in cinematic representation. After testing a third-person perspective on a smaller scale in *The Wind-Up Bird Chronicle*,

Murakami fully commits to it in his 1999 novel, *Sputnik Sweetheart (Supūtoniku no koibito)*. Murakami explains that writing *Sputnik Sweetheart* provided a chance to experiment with a new way of telling stories: "I think of *Sputnik* as a kind of experiment in style—a 'summation,' perhaps, or a 'leave taking,' or a 'fresh start.' I wanted to see how far I could go with a style in that book."[29] Murakami credits this change in his writing for the capacity of his later fiction to represent a larger perspective on the world.[30] Even as he incorporates a more objective viewpoint into his writing, Murakami seeks to uncover the dynamics of desire at the foundation of this perspective as a way of exposing the workings of the narrative gaze.

Instead of an omniscient voice originating outside the novel, then, *Sputnik Sweetheart* incorporates a third-person perspective that arises through the desire of characters-turned-narrators. The novel involves a love triangle told from the perspective of K, a schoolteacher, who serves as a mentor and confidant to a young novelist named Sumire, for whom he has a secret crush. However, his romantic interest goes unrequited, as Sumire is attracted to an older woman named Miu, a former concert pianist, who travels the world for business and hires Sumire as an assistant. At first, K honors his role as Sumire's mentor by acknowledging his function as the narrator of the story of which she is a part: "It's time to say a few words about myself. Of course this story is about Sumire, not me. Still, I'm the one whose eyes the story is told through—the tale of who Sumire is and what she did—and I should explain a little about the narrator. Me, in other words."[31] However, K's secret desire for Sumire causes him to daydream about her; she becomes a character in fantasies that gratify his desires to possess her, fantasies in which he serves as narrator as he does in the larger novel. This desire leads to the transformation of K's subjective voice into a third-person account that seeks to capture Sumire's life from a seemingly detached perspective, a perspective that arises from K's furtive desire for access to Sumire.[32]

The desire to see without being seen that K manifests calls to mind the dynamics of cinematic spectatorship at the basis of Sigmund Freud's notion of scopophilia—the pleasure of gazing at other people's bodies. Referencing Freud, critic Laura Mulvey identifies an impulse toward voyeurism in the workings of theatrical and cinematic spectatorship that are centered on an anonymous viewer who desires to gaze on an idealized version of themselves on-screen without being seen.[33] The experiences of Sumire's love interest, Miu, represents the impulse to project the self onto an observable other. Miu recalls an interaction with an older man named Ferdinando, who made unwanted romantic advances toward her during a summer she spent at the age of twenty-five in a small Swiss town. In a scene borrowed from a Virginia Woolf novel, one night, as she rides alone on a Ferris wheel overlooking the town, Miu catches a glimpse of her own house through her binoculars, and through her window, she sees herself in an intimate embrace with Ferdinando. The desire to both gaze upon an objectified subject and to identify with the subject one sees merges in an experience that replicates the act of watching a film in Miu's imagination.

The transformation of a personal perspective into an objective viewpoint is also a central way for characters to process trauma in Murakami's work. This transformation occurs because objective perspectives remove characters from distressing circumstances, situating them instead in safe positions as spectators of these scenarios, like Miu in the Ferris wheel example above.[34] In *1Q84*, one of the protagonists, Tengo, remembers a confusing moment from his childhood involving his mother's infidelity. Set in both 1984 Japan and an alternate version of that year, *1Q84* tracks the experiences of two star-crossed lovers, Tengo—a teacher and ghostwriter—and Aomame—a female assassin—as they seek to reunite while becoming embroiled in the machinations of a mysterious religious cult. To deal with the traumatic memory of his mother years later, Tengo recalls the experience from a detached position, as if he is watching a scene from a film. The third-person perspective allows him to sort through the memory:

Tengo's first memory dated from the time he was one and a half. His mother had taken off her blouse and dropped the shoulder straps of her white slip to let a man who was not his father suck on her breasts. The infant in the crib nearby was probably Tengo himself. He was observing the scene as a third person . . . if this memory of Tengo's was genuine, the scene must have been seared into his retinas as a pure image free of judgment—the way a camera records objects on film, mechanically, as a blend of light and shadow. And as his consciousness matured, the fixed image held in reserve would have been analyzed bit by bit, and meaning applied to it. But is such a thing even possible? Was the infant brain capable of preserving images like that?[35]

However, if the cinematic gaze serves as a way for characters to gain perspective on their lives, it also provides the means for them to escape the control levied by this same gaze. As a product of K's narrative imagination in *Sputnik Sweetheart*, Sumire becomes a character in his fantasy to possess her. Yet, as she grows in independence from K, Sumire also acquires the capacity to tell her own story, a process that Murakami describes using theatrical and cinematic metaphors that detail the way Sumire vanishes from K's field of vision. When Sumire disappears on a Greek island at the end of the novel, K loses track of her, describing his inability to narrate her story in terms of her function as a character on stage: "It was all so complicated, like something out of an existential play. Everything hit a dead end there, no alternatives left. And Sumire had exited stage right."[36] This exiting the stage, and the frame of K's narrative fantasy, indicate the development of Sumire's capacity to narrate her own story, a theme that is central to Murakami's work in the late 1990s and 2000s.[37]

The treatment of characters as objects of the gaze in Murakami's fiction takes on new meaning through the use of a camera apparatus as the main perspective in *After Dark*. Set during the hours from midnight to early morning, *After Dark* takes place in one of Tokyo's nighttime entertainment areas constantly under surveillance by the security cameras that monitor activity in the city. During this time, public transport to the outer suburbs ends, and those who are stuck downtown find shelter in dark corners of the city: all-night diners and seedy love hotels. In this panoptic setting, Mari, a college student, interacts with a diverse crew of characters, including Eri, her sister who sleeps for long stretches of time; Kaoru, the manager of a love hotel; and Shirakawa, a shady businessman and the central antagonist of the novel, who assaults a prostitute at the hotel where Kaoru works and who may be surveilling Eri using a camera secretly placed in her room to watch her while she sleeps.

Building on the motif of surveillance, Murakami utilizes a camera with the capacity to fly freely about in midair to track the movements of these characters, providing the reader a glimpse of the world without the mediation of a traditional narrator. The use of a camera as a narrator transforms readers into a viewer and the characters into objects of their gaze: "We allow ourselves to become a single point of view [in] the form of a midair camera that can move freely about the room."[38] As "pure point of view," this floating apparatus represents the full potential of cinematic representation, as Linda Hutcheon describes it: "More often we are told that the camera limits what we can see, eliminating the action on the periphery that might have caught our attention when watching a play on stage. . . . [However,] the use of cinematic techniques points to one of the major advantages films have over stage adaptations of novels: the use of a multitrack medium that, with the aid of the mediating camera, can both direct and expand the possibilities of perception."[39] Utilizing the language of cinematic movement, the opening of the novel provides the closest thing to a screenplay in Murakami's work.

> The camera draws back slowly to convey an image of the entire room. Then it begins observing details in search of clues. This is by no means a highly decorated room. Neither is it a room that suggests the tastes or individuality of its occupant. Without detailed observation, it would be hard to tell that this was the room of a young girl. . . . Once it has finished examining individual details, our viewpoint camera draws back momentarily and surveys the room once again. Then, as if unable to make up its mind, it maintains its broadened field of vision, its line of sight fixed in place for the time being. A pregnant silence reigns. At length, however, as if struck by a thought, it turns towards—and begins

to approach—a television set in a corner of the room: a perfectly square black Sony. The screen is dark, and as dead as the far side of the moon, but the camera seems to have sensed some kind of presence there—or perhaps a kind of foreshadowing. Wordlessly, we share this presence or foreshadowing with the camera as we stare at the screen in close-up.[40]

Barbara Greene draws attention to the cinematic nature of the diction in the passage: "From the first page, the narrator acts almost as a film director, describing the activities and the environment as if they were the storyboard of or the table read for a movie."[41]

The intimate voice describing the images captured by the floating camera, furthermore, collapses the distance between the apparatus and the viewer's perspective by claiming to provide a neutral viewpoint. This viewpoint allows the reader to observe the external details without delving into the psychology of characters. It addresses the reader in the first-person plural—"we"—indicating that the viewer is present and seeing what the narrator sees rather than hearing it secondhand: "Our point of view, as an imaginary camera, picks up and lingers over things like this in the room. We are invisible, anonymous intruders. We look. We listen. We note odours. But we are not physically present in the place, and we leave behind no traces. We follow the same rules, so to speak, as orthodox time travelers. We observe but we do not intervene."[42]

If the reader merges with the filmic apparatus in the passages mentioned above, characters transform into cinematic images as they are tracked by the roaming perspective of the camera. After setting the scene, the camera focuses its attention on Eri as she sleeps soundly in her room like Snow White: "At the moment, the camera is situated directly above the bed and is focused on her sleeping face. . . . Eri goes on sleeping in the single bed in the center of the room. We recognize the bed and the bedclothes. We approach her and study her face while she sleeps, taking time to observe the details with great care."[43] The projection of characters as cinematic images blurs boundaries between image and original, adding to the hyperreal nature of the narration.[44] The narrative perspective describing the mysterious businessman Shirakawa takes on a life of its own when he looks into a mirror:

Shirakawa inspects his face in the mirror. The muscles of his face remain immobile as he stares at himself long and hard with severe eyes. His hands rest on the sink. He holds his breath and never blinks, fully expecting that, if he were to stay like this long enough, some other thing might emerge. To objectify all the senses, to flatten the consciousness, to put a temporary freeze on logic, to bring the advance of time to a halt if only momentarily—this is what he is trying to do: to fuse his being with the scene behind him, to make everything look like a neutral still life. Try as he might to suppress his own presence, that other thing never emerges. His image in the mirror remains just that: an image of himself in reality. A reflection of what is there. He gives up, takes a deep breath, filling his lungs with new air, and straightens his posture. . . . The door closes. Even after Shirakawa has left, our point of view remains in the lavatory, and, as a stationary camera, continues to capture the dark mirror. Shirakawa's reflection is still there in the mirror. Shirakawa—or perhaps we should say his image—is looking in this direction from within the mirror. It does not move or change expression. It simply stares straight ahead. Eventually, however, as though giving up, it relaxes, takes a deep breath, and rolls its head. Then it brings its hand to its face and rubs its cheek a few times, as if checking for the touch of flesh.[45]

Having demonstrated the way cinematic representation has shaped Murakami's work in the last twenty years, the balance of this chapter and book focuses on the other side of the relationship: how Murakami has influenced global cinema. That Murakami's fiction deals with issues that are central to the workings of filmic expression could be part of the reason why so many adaptations of his work have emerged over the last thirty years. Although Murakami is closely invested in the translation of his literary fiction into different languages, he is not as involved in the process of adapting his stories into film, apart from granting permission to filmmakers interested in using his work.[46] However, as films based on Murakami's writing continue to be released, a tension between two competing impulses emerges in these works: a desire to relay Murakami's distinctive style in cinematic form, which seeks to preserve meaning in his works that exists prior to the adaptation process, and an inclination to expand the scope of his fiction, which suggests that meaning is a product of the adaptation process itself rather than something preexisting it.

We see this tension in one of the first adaptations of Murakami's writing, *Hear the Song of the Wind* by Ōmori. Initially, the film feels like a homage to the author and his first novella, reproducing Murakami's iconic first-person perspective through a point-of-view sequence of the narrator as he travels from Tokyo to Kobe and makes his way to Jay's Bar when he arrives in town. Throughout the film, voice-overs reading directly from the source text frame the action, allowing viewers to hear Murakami's distinctive voice. The film occasionally uses intertitles of quotes from the novel that serve as informal chapter markers, giving shape to the developing story while grounding the film in Murakami's writing. To capture the fragmented structure of the novel, furthermore, the film utilizes flashbacks, freeze-frames, animated sequences, cutaways to objects and advertisements, and other techniques. Sound is also used to tie the world of the film to the author's

Figure 1.1. A point-of-view shot from *Hear the Wind Sing* captures Murakami's first-person perspective.

彼女は間違っている。

Figure 1.2. A quote from Murakami's novel *Hear the Wind Sing* recaptured in cinematic adaptation.

work. Whether emanating from the jukebox in Jay's Bar, the stereo at a record shop, or the radio, songs referenced in the novel, like the Beach Boys' "California Girls," play throughout the film, recreating the atmosphere of early 1970s Japan that Murakami captures in his writing.

Yet, even as they acknowledge the author's position at the center of these stories, cinematic adaptations also produce something new. Before we analyze the different adaptations of Murakami's work, it is important to outline some of the ideas related to transmedia storytelling that will frame our discussion. Transmedia storytelling refers to the transfer of narrative meaning from one medium or platform to another—from literature to film, for instance. Stories gain meaning as they move across multiple media platforms, with each platform making unique contributions to the story world. For instance, the Harry Potter universe expands as the story moves between the mediums of literature, film, drama, and even theme parks, motivating fans to track the story as it develops across these different platforms.

Although the transmedia landscape of Murakami's work is continually increasing to include film, television, drama, and other media, this book will primarily focus on transmedia storytelling between literature, film, and animation. It will concentrate particularly on the adaptation of Murakami's fiction into feature films and shorts, using terminology like "source text" or "original" to refer to Murakami's own authored works of literature, "cinematic adaptation" to refer to the product that results from the transposition of stories from source texts to the medium of film, "context" to describe the different historical and cultural settings in which adaptations occur, and "fidelity" or "faithfulness" to refer to the relationship between the source text and the cinematic adaptation. While adaptations are often judged based on their fidelity to the source text—their ability to faithfully translate the characters, plot, setting, and specifics of the original story—Hutcheon argues that adaptations should also be judged on their ability to create something new in the process. Describing adaptation as a "*process of creation*," Hutcheon argues that "the act of adaptation always involves both (re-)interpretation and then (re-) creation."[47] "Perhaps one way to think about unsuccessful adaptations," she writes, "is not in terms of infidelity to a prior text, but in terms of the lack of creativity and skill to make the text one's own and thus autonomous."[48]

This type of evaluation even applies to films that closely reference Murakami as an auteur, like *Hear the Song of the Wind*. Though faithful to the source text early on, the film draws out issues that are not prominently featured in the original. Hidden beneath the surface of the atmosphere of apathy in the novel, the violent student movements of the 1960s and early 1970s are explored more extensively in the film. Ōmori shows more interest than Murakami in developing the historical and political landscape of the time in order to flesh out the experience of the student movements in Japan, which he also experienced as a contemporary of Murakami.[49] Flashbacks to the violence of the student movements play throughout the film, often creating a contrast to the mundane reality of the narrator's life. During the title sequence, an impressionistic montage of footage from violent demonstrations in Tokyo is accompanied by a soundtrack of chaotic jazz music. A shaky camera captures the unsettling images of fires burning in the streets while police in riot

Figure 1.3. *Hear the Wind Sing* gestures towards
a larger history behind the novel.

Figure 1.4. *Hear the Wind Sing* gestures towards
a larger history behind the novel.

gear descend on the crowds. The implications of these images are given greater impact through a montage of tumultuous events from around the world in the 1960s, like the Kennedy assassination, which plays partway through the film.

In this way, a creative impulse in the adaptation of *Hear the Wind Sing* expands the transmedia landscape of this Murakami story by developing the historical context that gives it shape, delving into some of the details of the world in which the story takes place that the source text does not depict. Though this view of adaptation as a creative act seems to invite us to move beyond the value of fidelity in evaluating a cinematic adaptation, this book argues that the very creative nature of adaptation is paradoxically faithful to Murakami's writing and to Haruki World by virtue of its capacity to revitalize our way of reading his literature and reflect the process that Murakami himself uses to create his fiction. Creative adaptations, as this book argues, replicate a central technique of Murakami's writing itself, particularly his more surreal works: the way his stories continually seek to transform our view of characters, narrative perspectives, settings, and even ontological experiences into something new. Like these stories, the cinematic adaptations similarly blend and merge narrative elements, themes, and characters to provide a new perspective on the meaning and implications of Murakami's work itself within the different contexts in which it is read.

The following chapters will develop this argument through an analysis of films based on Murakami's work produced over the last forty years. Chapter two will argue that the time and distance separating adaptations from source texts like "The Bakery Attack" and "The Second Bakery Attack" enable filmmakers to escape the interpretive context surrounding these literary works. This separation allows filmmakers to speak to specific conditions around the world while also creating new connections to source texts by renewing ways of reading them. Chapter three describes the way Murakami's "Drive My Car" depicts the central role translation plays in creating meaning in Murakami's work. The chapter focuses on Hamaguchi's adaptation, *Drive My Car*, and its attention to its own act of "translating" from one medium to another, from a literary work to stage and screen. Just as the act of adaptation opens up literary texts, projecting them onto the stage and the diegetic world of cinema, the work of translating and adapting Murakami, a prominent translator of American fiction himself, lays bare the makeup of his stories, revealing them to be a collection of references to other literary works rather than hermeneutically sealed stories. Lee's *Burning*, for instance, offers a look not only into the influences acting on Murakami's work but also to Murakami's own role as a translator by citing the stories and novels that influenced "Barn Burning," specifically William Faulkner's story by the same name and F. Scott Fitzgerald's *The Great Gatsby*. Chapters four and five analyze the way the formal attributes of film and animation renew our understanding of Murakami's stories while replicating the process of writing them. As recent films like *Norwegian Wood* and *Burning* suggest, depicting Murakami's stories through film focuses attention away from ontological issues that are often highlighted in the interpretations of his stories and turns it toward temporal concerns. Experiencing Murakami's stories as an expression of time sheds greater light on their ability to speak to a shared experience with modernization in Asia. Finally, chapter five concludes the discussion by examining the way the very act of blending Murakami stories through hybrid animation techniques and narrative inventiveness reflects Murakami's own literary project to blend characters, storylines, genres, and even modes of representation in his work.

# 2

# Crime on Camera: Screening "The Bakery Attack"

This chapter focuses on the adaptations of Murakami Haruki's most influential series of stories: "The Bakery Attack" (1981) and its sequel, "The Second Bakery Attack" (1985). The stories have been adapted by Japanese director Yamakawa Naoto in 1982, South Korean director You Sang-Hun in 2010, Mexican director Carlos Cuarón in 2010, and Polish director Michal Wawrzecki in 2014. Reflecting the entropic forces of globalization, these different versions of the stories have developed independently from their source texts over the last thirty-five years, moving beyond the milieu of 1970s and 1980s Japan to address issues related to the historical and cultural contexts in which they were produced. And yet, by teasing out aspects of Murakami's work that are overlooked in standard readings of his stories, these adaptations renew our understanding of the source texts by cutting through the layers of interpretation that have calcified around them over time. In doing so, they demonstrate the way adaptations form connections to original works by revitalizing our interpretations of these stories notwithstanding their temporal and geographical separation from them.

Murakami's stories "The Bakery Attack" and "The Second Bakery Attack" have been released in various forms since the inception of the series in the early 1980s. "The Bakery Attack" first appeared in the literary journal *Waseda Bungaku* in 1981 and was released in the collection of Murakami's short stories, *Let's Meet in Our Dreams* (*Yume de aimashō*), the same year. "The Second Bakery Attack" was first published in the Japanese-language edition of the French magazine *Marie Claire* in 1985. It was later reprinted in the short story collection *The Second Bakery Attack* (*Pan'ya saishūgeki*) in 1986 and in *The Complete Works of Murakami Haruki 1980–1991* (*Murakami Haruki zen sakuhin shū 1980–1991*) in 1991. A translation of "The Second Bakery Attack" by Jay Rubin was subsequently published in 1993 in *The Elephant Vanishes*, the first collection of English-language translations of Murakami's short stories. In 2013, Murakami released new versions of both stories, renamed "Attack the Bakery" ("Panya wo osō") and "Attacking the Bakery, Again" ("Futatabi panya o osō"), in an illustrated collection named *Panya wo osō*.

Notwithstanding these many iterations of the stories, many of their general plot points have remained the same over time. Set in the mid-1970s, "The Bakery Attack" tells of two hungry students, the narrator and his friend, who decide to rob a bakery run by a communist bread maker. The overwhelming craving for physical sustenance that drives the two students to criminal behavior manifests their urge for self-realization and purpose in a world in which "God, Marx, and John Lennon are all dead," as the protagonist suggests. Wielding a knife, the two enter a bakery located on a suburban shopping street—the kind of which there are many in Japan—only to have their plans frustrated by a middle-aged female customer ahead of them in line who takes an inordinate amount of time choosing bakery items. When the two would-be thieves finally reach the register and confront the baker, they are taken aback by his proposition to them. He tells them that instead of stealing bread, they can have as much as they like. All they must do in return is listen to the music of Richard Wagner with him, thereby gaining an appreciation for the works of the German composer (1813–1883). The two go along with the baker's proposal, and the story ends with them listening to the Wagner opera *Tristan and Isolde* while wolfing down bread to their hearts' content.

"The Second Bakery Attack" picks up with the narrator of "The Bakery Attack" a decade later. Now in his late twenties, the narrator is married and works at a Tokyo law firm. Late one night, he is once again struck by the same overwhelming hunger that he experienced ten years earlier. As he and his wife, who also feels the hunger, search through the apartment for something to eat, he relays to her the story of the first attack and his regret for compromising with the baker. His choice to listen to Wagner in exchange for bread, the narrator believes, has left him with a curse all these years later. As a visual manifestation of this curse, the narrator imagines throughout the story that he is in a boat floating on the ocean directly above an underwater volcano that is ready to explode. Driven by their hunger, the two head out into the Tokyo streets in the middle of the night, eventually deciding to steal hamburgers at McDonald's because they are unable to find a bakery open at that hour. As they ready themselves for the assault, the narrator is surprised to find that his wife has prepared Remington shotguns and ski masks to aid them in the crime. Moving with "trained efficiency," she also covers their car's license plates with self-adhesive tape. Brandishing the shotguns, they burst into the McDonald's and demand thirty Big Macs. The manager initially refuses to hand over the burgers, offering instead to give the couple money to avoid issues with accounting.

Nevertheless, they insist, and he delivers up the burgers in bags. The couple snatch the burgers, and some Cokes, which they pay for, and make their way to an empty parking lot, where they consume their loot while watching the sunrise.

Critics largely interpret the Bakery Attack series as a commentary on the postrevolutionary mood of Japan after the end of the extremist era of the late 1960s and early 1970s. During the extremist era, activists sought progress and equality by pushing to reform educational and government institutions. While many activists, like those who belonged to the Japanese Communist Party (JCP), encouraged peaceful demonstrations, others advocated more violent forms of resistance. Confrontations grew aggressive in 1968, as activists aimed to inspire revolution by initiating violent clashes with police, spurring a heavy crackdown on radical groups. In 1969, the Red Army Faction (Sekigun-ha) was formed by activist icon Shigenobu Fusako with the goal of overthrowing the government and sparking an uprising. The Red Army Faction went underground soon after it was formed as a result of police repression, splitting into three groups, one that escaped to North Korea, another to the Middle East (which included Shigenobu), and a third that stayed in Japan. Those that remained in Japan merged with other militant groups—including the Revolutionary Left—to form the United Red Army (URA; Rengō sekigun). On February 17, 1971, three members of the URA, wearing ski masks, robbed a gun shop in the Tochigi Prefecture, making off with ten Remington shotguns, an air rifle, and 2,400 rounds of ammunition. Authorities found their ski masks in an abandoned automobile that was equipped with fake license plates.[1] Hounded by authorities, the URA eventually imploded shortly after the robbery, marking the end of the radical period and the start of an era of economic prosperity. "The reform movement that captured much of the vitality of the early postwar decades," critics Gavin McCormick and Meredith Box suggest, "was either foreclosed, as many were co-opted in the 'all-for growth' economism, consumerism, and the corporation, or crushed in successive waves of repression of dissidence as the cold war order took shape."[2]

Critics identify references in "The Bakery Attack" to the culture of 1960s activism. The language used by the protagonist and his friend—including terms like "ware ware" ("we"), "tēze" ("thesis"), and "seimei" ("declaration")—call to mind the slogans of groups like Zengakuren, the league of associated student activists.[3] Likewise, the conflict between the two characters and a communist baker alludes to the fallout between the JCP and members of Zengakuren during this time.[4] Though these two groups initially worked together to fight for leftist causes, a rift developed between them due to philosophical differences: the students wanted drastic change while the JCP sought less radical measures in realizing their goals. Mori Masaki comments on the contrast the story creates between the more aggressive activists and the complacent JCP: "The student movement in the late sixties ideologically veered toward the left in reaction to the conservative government, although it functioned largely independent of any direct party control, which explains the mocking, discrediting portrayal of the bald baker in his fifties as an unlikely, ineffectual communist who, content with his small business, admiringly listens to Wagner in tedium."[5]

Although seemingly headed for a violent conclusion, the conflict eventually leads to compromise. The attackers get what they need but only by agreeing to listen to Wagner. Though an ostensibly innocuous request, this deal robs the two of their capacity to challenge the system. While listening to music does not constitute "labor" in the pure sense of the word, the protagonist reasons, he nevertheless acknowledges a "grave mistake" in commodifying his labor in this business-like transaction, allowing them to be absorbed into the logic of capitalist exchange (listening to Wagner for bread), the very logic they resisted. The use of Wagner, moreover, has significance in the overall context of the failure of revolution, argues Katō Norihiro: "Wagner's opera at the bakery symbolizes canonized music and, as such, the established social order or discourse. Acquiescing to accept the composition signifies [becoming] part of the system, unknowingly succumbing oneself to its yoke at the expense of a young aspiration to be rebellious and independent."[6] In the end, prioritizing material gratification over the long-term goal of economic equality leaves the protagonist with a curse he cannot shake.

"The Second Bakery Attack" builds on the history of activism referenced in "The Bakery Attack" to frame the student movements within the prosperity of Japan's bubble economy in the 1980s. Reading the two stories together sheds light on the disorienting effects of the transition between these two eras. The mid-1980s, when the second story is set, signifies a time of great economic growth, creating a divide between it and the early 1980s, when the memory of anti-capitalist movements in the early 1970s was not yet extinguished by prosperity. To accentuate this time lag, the events of "The Bakery Attack" are described in "The Second Bakery Attack" as having taken place ten years earlier. This would place them in the mid-1970s, just after the end of the revolutionary movements but close enough that, as Mori suggests, "the reminisced original attack could coincide with the period when the effects of the student movements were still at least felt . . . and Japan was yet to attain the apex of its unprecedented economic prosperity."[7] The protagonist of "The Second Bakery Attack" manifests the estrangement that results from a sudden shift from Marxist to capitalistic values. In contrast to the youthful ambition and idealism of the narrator of "The Bakery Attack," the narrator of the sequel has become a jaded consumer in the space of ten years. This abrupt turn away from Marxism to capitalist prosperity reflects a fractured sense of identity. Many of Murakami's protagonists—including the narrator of "The Bakery Attack"—and the larger generation they represent experience this fragmented identity, as the disillusioned narrator of the 1992 novel, *South of the Border, West of the Sun*, suggests:

> After all, I was part of the generation that spawned the radical student movement. We were the first to yell a resounding "No!" at the logic of late capitalism, which had devoured any remaining post-war ideals. It was like the outbreak of a fever just as the country stood at a crucial turning point. And here I was myself, swallowed up by the very same capitalist logic, as I lounged in my BMW, waiting for the lights to change at a crossroads in ritzy Tokyo. I was living someone else's life, not my own. How much of this person I called myself was actually me? And how much was not?[8]

Although thoroughly immersed in Japan's bubble economy, the narrator of "The Second Bakery Attack" is nevertheless unable to completely move on from the 1970s. Employed at a law firm, he is in the early stages of forming his own nuclear family unit, the kind that served as a social safety net for economic growth during this time. The ideal postwar family in Japan in the 1980s was composed of a hierarchical relationship among a father who provided for the family, a mother who cared for the home, and the children. This family unit was expected to carry the burden of societal advancement.[9] Neoliberal policy viewed the family as a "substitute" for the welfare state and "the primary source of economic security."[10] Families were expected to relieve the country of the financial burden of providing for its citizens' welfare by taking care of their own. Fully onboard with this new culture of prosperity, the narrator grows out of touch with the part of himself that fought so fiercely against the values he now embraces. The choice to compromise in his earlier days has divided the activist and consumerist sides of his identity, keeping him from developing into a coherent individual. As a result, the hunger he felt before returns with irrational consequences.

The magical realism of "The Second Bakery Attack" accentuates the disorientating effects of the transformation of Japan during the 1970s and 1980s. Magical realism constitutes a mode of writing that mobilizes the conventions of setting, character, and plot to faithfully represent the reality of everyday life while introducing extraordinary events that are not explained by science or logic. To enhance their defamiliarizing effects, magical realist stories are set in everyday locations with ordinary people as characters—the more mundane, the better. This everydayness disarms the reader, signaling to them that they are in a familiar world, making the magical intrusion into this safe realm all the more impactful. Furthermore, when a touch of the fantastic does arise in this world, it is narrated in a straightforward, matter-of-fact manner that goes against the reader's expectation for the narrator to make sense of the bizarreness of the incidents. Murakami critics like Strecher advocate using the idea of magical realism to account for the strange events that occur within the realistic worlds that Murakami creates in his fiction.[11]

The everydayness of the setting of "The Second Bakery Attack" provides the basis for the more fantastic events that occur. These fantastic events seemingly lack a purpose when the story is encountered as a stand-alone work. Yet, when considered in relation to the narrator's original experience (which is referenced in the story), these uncanny plot details work to defamiliarize the 1980s in Japan, reflecting the feelings of schizophrenia that resulted from the abrupt change in the cultural landscape. The city streets and shopping districts in the sequel conform to the real-world geographical layout of Tokyo with which readers would be familiar, and the characters are the very people one would expect to inhabit a McDonald's early in the morning: late-night staff and patrons on an all-night bender. And yet, within this very ordinary world, uncanny happenings occur. The wife's trained efficiency in carrying out the robbery, seemingly odd in a country with such strict gun regulations, alludes to the Tochigi gun robbery and the iconic women of the activist movement, like Shigenobu Fusako. The emergence of these anachronistic details within the mundane routines of everyday life indicates the persistence of unreconciled experiences from the recent past that have been suppressed beneath the prosperity of the bubble period. These strange happenings invite the reader to look beyond the dominant understanding of contemporary Japan as an advanced, rational, and efficient nation to consider how events that do not fit this narrative are marginalized to tell it. In this way, the relationship between the two historical periods treated in the series provides context for the uncanny events in the second story, relaying the disorienting experience of student radicalism and its aftermath.

That the cinematic adaptations of the Bakery Attack series focus on one of the two source texts, not both, deemphasizes the connection between the two original works while teasing out new resonances that go beyond their standard interpretations. Two films from East Asian directors—Yamakawa Naoto's 1982 short, Attack on a Bakery (Pan'ya shūgeki), and part two of South Korean director You Sang-Hun's 2010 omnibus feature, Acoustic (Eokuseutig)—provide differing views of the effects of the student movements in Japan and South Korea through their treatment of the first story. Yamakawa's Attack on a Bakery, which was released the same year as Murakami's "The Second Bakery Attack," focuses on the Marxist rhetoric used in "The Bakery Attack" while lacking the context and added meaning provided by the second story and its emphasis on the disillusionment and displacement experienced after the end of the movements. Instead, the film reignites the anger of late 1960s activism. A contemporary of Murakami, Yamakawa secured the rights to make the film through his younger sister, who worked at the jazz bar Murakami ran before he became a full-time writer.[12] Cinematic devices accentuate the Marxist implications of the story, foregrounding its ideological dimension. The film opens with the protagonist and his friend philosophizing about their hunger. A disembodied voice-over reads the narrator's pontifications on the emptiness of consumer society, cutting to reveal the two protagonists lying on the floor of their small apartment. That the voice-over reads directly from the source text does not allow for ambiguity between the visuals presented on screen and the anti-capitalist rhetoric. Foreshadowing the violent implications of their hunger, the camera captures a poster for the Japanese gangster film series *Battles without Honor and Humanity* (*Jingi naki tatakai* [1973–1974]) by Fukusaku Kinji (1930–2003) hanging in the background. The first installment of the five-part docudrama tells of the dog-eat-dog culture of yakuza gangs in Hiroshima after World War II. Mimicking their violent efforts for survival, the two protagonists grab a knife and head down to the bakery.

As the action shifts to the bakery, the cinematic framing and intertitles accentuate the film's anti-capitalist message. Though bread provides necessary sustenance for life, the bakery emerges as a symbol of the ills of the market economy. It is captured in a wide shot, accentuating the power it has over the characters, while a series of POV quick cuts pull the viewer into its doors, emphasizing how naturally one is drawn into the trappings of consumerism. The consequences of capitalism—material excess and class division—are accentuated beyond the meaning of the original story through a depiction of the female customer played by Yamakawa's college friend, the actress Muroi Shigeru. As in the original story, the woman struggles to decide what to purchase as she holds a tray with three bakery items, suggesting the tyranny of choice introduced by a consumer economy. Perhaps reading too much into the meaning of the bread, Katō argues that the three pieces correspond to the three sectors of Japanese industry: farming and fishing, construction and manufacturing, and service and information. At this moment in history, Katō suggests, Japan was in the process of shifting to the third sector.[13] This reference to the development of advanced capitalism is followed by a pointed critique of its implications in the next shot, as the screen divides into three panels, one depicting the woman living in poverty, another showing her standing in the bakery, and the final one revealing her as a member of the wealthy elite. This tryptic illustration of class division suggests that like excess, social discord is a natural consequence of economic progress. Meaning is further imposed onto the visuals through the use of intertitles that function as subliminal messaging: the word "excess" flashes for a few seconds in between shots of the woman. Other terms like "uniformity" and "unification of the unconscious" also appear on-screen. According to the booklet that accompanies the DVD version of the film, the words on the intertitles are common slogans that were written on signs used by student protestors during the movements.

Figure 2.1. A customer struggles to choose bread in *Attack on a Bakery*.

The ideological conditioning continues as the two protagonists return to their apartment. In a scene that does not appear in the source text, one protagonist repeatedly hits the wall of his apartment with his fist, seemingly unsatisfied by the encounter at the bakery. This action disturbs his neighbor—an older gentleman in sunglasses—who asks him to be quiet. The DVD booklet suggests that the sunglasses reference Japanese biker gangs (*bōsōzoku*), who espoused more conservative values in contrast to the progressive student activists. Giving in to the demands of the biker is yet another instance of acquiescence to the conservative status quo that leftist revolutionaries fought so hard to resist. This residual anger is reflected in the final slogan that flashes on-screen at the very end of the film: "down with democracy!" As the message appears, the frame closes in a circular shape around the protagonist's face, eventually wiping to a black screen as the film ends. This strong anti-capitalist message is enabled by a decontextualized reading of the first story as an independent work, one that lacks the perspective provided by the sequel. It draws attention to the political anger that resides in the subtext of the first story—anger that is concealed by feelings of displacement and disillusionment that come through when the two stories are read together.

The film *Acoustic* uses "The Bakery Attack" to reconcile the experiences of the postrevolutionary milieu in South Korea, which occurred a decade after the movements in Japan. Directed by You Sang-Hun, *Acoustic* depicts the lives of young

Figure 2.2. A triptych composition in *Attack on a Bakery*.

Figure 2.3. Intertitles reproduce slogans from the
student movements in *Attack on a Bakery*.

adults making music in the Hongdae area of contemporary Seoul. The first of the three sections of the film involves a terminally ill singer determined to share her final song with the world, while the third episode is set in a distant postapocalyptic future and involves a couple searching for a lost iPhone that contains music from their youth. Based on "The Bakery Attack," the second vignette tells of two Seoul youth trying to make it as a musical act. However, unlike Yamakawa's *Attack on a Bakery*, which captures the anger and ideological spirit of the revolutionary movements, being less than a decade removed from them, the perspective presented in *Acoustic* is further detached from the counterculture of the late 1960s in Japan and the 1980s in South Korea. While activism in the 1960s was led by baby boomers around the world, the student movements in South Korea were directed by the 386 generation, the cohort of Marxist proponents that emerged in the 1980s amidst the socioeconomic transformations of society. The name of this generation refers to both Intel's 386 computer, which was introduced in the mid-1980s during the movements, as well as to people then in their 30s who, attending university in the 80s, were raised in the 60s—hence, "386." Modernization during this time led to several social changes in South Korea: the depletion of a rural workforce and the development of deplorable conditions at factories and other industrial centers. Reactionary movements resulted in several violent demonstrations in which students were injured and killed. Marxist activities were eventually suppressed by the authoritarian government, which recognized all forms of dissidence as pro-communist. As with other revolutionary cohorts around the world, members of the 386 generation went on to become part of the elite of South Korean society in the 1990s, retaining their liberal values while also benefiting from the same trappings of a consumer society that they resisted as Marxist revolutionaries. After their country embraced state-sponsored capitalism, they experienced the same disillusionment and angst that Murakami's characters express, so it is only natural that the 386 generation would be drawn to Murakami's work, as Kim Choon-mie argues:

> It is easy to see why [Murakami's] novels, depicting as they do the sense of failure and loss that Japanese youths experienced in . . . the transition to consumer capitalism, were eagerly accepted in South Korea. Korean youths who were born in the 1960s and committed themselves to student protests in the 1980s . . . were stricken with a sense of lethargy and emptiness after having realized a regime change. Murakami's works perfectly echoed the anguish of these youths, the loss of ideology in the course of late capitalist society's shift away from politics and history, the appetite for consumption that filled the void, and the ambience of a vain, affluent, society.[14]

Like the source text, You's *Acoustic* references student movements from the past. Yet, instead of angst and disillusionment, the film depicts the enduring communality of the 386 generation, suggesting that the values they espoused persist in contemporary times. More than any other adaptation of Murakami's work, the second section of *Acoustic* takes creative license in reworking aspects of the original story to fit a new context. Music and baked goods are still linked in the film, but they take on new meaning in a story about the adventures of Seong-won and Hae-won, members of a two-man band who struggle to make money performing gigs at venues around Seoul. To make ends meet, they make the difficult decision to sell one of their beloved guitars. On the way to the transaction, Seong-won stops at a bakery (he is hungry because Hae-won did not share the noodles he ate for lunch), only to realize he has no money. However, the sympathetic owner of the bakery offers him some bread, telling him to pay only what he can afford. After wolfing down the food, Seong-won leaves the bakery to meet up with the person to whom he arranged to sell the guitar, only to realize that he left it in the bakery. Later, Seong-won returns to the bakery with Hae-won, and the two question the owner, who claims to know nothing about the missing guitar. Growing suspicious, the two friends demand the return of their property. It turns out, however, that the guitar was placed in the back by a staff member. Angered by the duo's greed, the baker lectures them on what it really means to love music. While offering them some of his bread, he fixes their guitar strings, which were broken during the encounter, and then uses the same guitar to play a well-known folk ballad for them, revealing himself to be its songwriter.

Treating music and bread not as commodities but as things freely given, *Acoustic* tempers the anger of the original story, "The Bakery Attack." This adaptation helps reconcile the prosperity of the 386 generation in the years following the movements in the 1990s with the Marxist values they espoused in the 1980s. Steeped in the trappings of capitalism, Hae-won and Seong-won represent the children of the 1990s, those who grew up amidst South Korea's prosperity. Hunger in the film represents an excess of desire that emerges from the emphasis placed on economic privatization, as both Hae-won and Seong-won greedily hoard food, refusing to share with each other. However, as the film suggests, the communal spirit nevertheless persists, resisting the greed unleashed by capitalism. Fittingly, it is a member of the 386 generation who reintroduces these values into the world. Approximating the age of members of this cohort, the baker blends the values of both the student revolutionaries and the prosperous professionals they would become. Although a successful business owner, he nevertheless encourages collectivity and equality, giving freely of his bread to Seong-won and Hae-won. Music becomes a symbol for the enduring purity of the communal values of the 386 generation that are still alive even in the second decade of the twenty-first century. Inspired by the baker's generosity, Hae-won and Seong-won take their act

Figure 2.4. The baker plays a song in *Acoustic*.

Figure 2.5. The duo plays a free concert for the public in *Acoustic*.

to the street, performing their music for free in front of a large crowd that gathers around them. In contrast to the claustrophobic cinematography that captures their performance at the start of the vignette, the band is framed in wide shots, as the camera gently pulls out to reveal the crowd forming around them.

Notwithstanding the way Murakami's work resonates with the 386 generation, the adaptation of "The Bakery Attack" in a South Korean context reveals subtle differences between the moods following the student movements in Japan and South Korea. Whereas the Bakery Attack series emphasizes the disorienting effects of moving from resistance to complicity in such a short period of time, *Acoustic* portrays a South Korean cultural consciousness that is not as alienated from its history, suggesting that the economic growth the country worked so hard to achieve has not erased a desire for the collective spirit of the past.

While adaptations of the Bakery Attack series that emerge in Asia tend to focus on the first story, films outside of East Asia favor "The Second Bakery Attack" as source material. This choice among filmmakers is due to the lack of an English-language translation of "The Bakery Attack." Additionally, the second story is more accessible to global audiences, with its contemporary setting and understated treatment of the student movements in Japan, a historical event with which readers outside of Asia would not be acquainted. Because interpretations of the stories focus so heavily on activism, moving attention away from this historical moment allows other issues to come to the forefront, challenging the primacy of these interpretations in the first place.

Accordingly, Carlos Cuarón's 2010 short film, *The Second Bakery Attack*, adapts the source text to speak to issues in contemporary America, allowing the socioeconomic critique in Murakami's writing to take on new meaning as it is adapted in a different society. Apart from some minor plot details, the overall feel of the story matches the original, highlighting the universal applicability of Murakami's writing. Cuarón argues this point in an interview with CNN: "[The film is] short, but there's meticulous attention to detail just like a Murakami story! . . . To me, Murakami's works are universal, and at the same time very Japanese. This is what makes the project so intriguing for me—I did set the story in the United States but the tone of the conversations, the situation . . . somehow it's very Tokyo."[15] Instead of Tokyo in the 1980s, the film is set in an average American town around the year 2010. The young Japanese couple is replaced by an American one, Nat and Dan, played by Kirsten Dunst and Brian Geraghty. The newly married couple have a fight, which is exacerbated by an overwhelming hunger that keeps them both awake one night. Because the events of the first story are not shown in flashback but only alluded to in conversation between the couple, the historical link to the past is less significant than it is in the original series. Likewise, the wife explains away the presence of her shotgun by telling her husband that it belonged to her grandfather, thus eliminating the defamiliarizing effects of the original. Though something similar did happen years ago, the film suggests, the connection to the past is not important.

Instead, the film draws the viewer's attention to the here and now, to the more pressing political issues with which the United States grappled in 2010. One of these issues, racial politics, becomes the focus of the film. Gitte Marianne Hansen and Michael Tsang suggest, "The film highlights America's own intricate issue of racial politics, and accordingly makes several obvious changes in the film to foreground it."[16] For example, Cuarón's choice of Caucasian actors to play the couple robbing the restaurant, and Latino and Black actors as staff, they argue, challenges some of the stereotypical views of racial minorities in America. That the criminals are played by white actors, and the victims of the crime by minorities, attempts to reverse the "criminal Black man" myth, a myth that refers to the way the media often "stereotypically portrays the African American male as the dangerous criminal."[17] While the Caucasian actors brandish a shotgun, the staff act as consummate professionals, treating them like paying customers.

However, Hansen and Tsang's analysis of racial politics in the film ignores an issue that sheds further light on the significance of the treatment of race. Viewed in the context of the Great Recession at the end of the first decade of the 2000s—the most severe economic recession in the United States since the Great Depression of the 1930s—the film demonstrates the role white privilege plays in realizing economic security. The recession began when the housing market in the United States went bust and large amounts of mortgage-backed securities lost significant value. During the recession, US GDP declined by 0.3 percent in 2008 and 2.8 percent in 2009 while unemployment reached 10 percent. This economic crisis spread worldwide, leading to a global financial catastrophe in 2009 that particularly impacted the younger generation because it led to the decline of the employment and housing markets just as this generation began looking to secure jobs and purchase homes. The desperation of the young couple in the film reflects the plight of this economically vulnerable demographic. And yet, what Cuarón is drawing our attention to is the disproportionate way the recession impacted ethnic minorities and members of the working class, many of whom lost their homes due to the economic downturn. Though the recession was a challenge to the middle class, devaluing their 401(k)s and even leading to unemployment, it was even more devastating for those on the bottom rung of the socioeconomic ladder. These people became victims not only of the recession but also of those of the upper class, who were fighting tooth and nail to retain their wealth.

Racial and class lines are drawn around the idea of the house in the film, the symbol of what was lost during the economic downturn. It is significant that the only characters shown with a home are the young Caucasian couple; the restaurant staff, all ethnic minorities, are working the late shift. Though seized with hunger, moreover, the young couple has mobility: they leave their house in the middle of the night to rob the restaurant, while the staff is held hostage in the kitchen to cook for them. This critique of white middle-class entitlement is compounded by the superficial wokeness of the young couple, who recognize the cultural imperialism of American burger joints like McDonald's (referred to as "America Burger" in the film). "It's better to attack an America Burger," the wife suggests, "fucking imperialist pigs." Yet, even as they embrace more progressive politics, they are out of touch with the issues of inequality at home, using Spanish words like "*amigo*" and "*gracias*" in a culturally insensitive way when demanding their food. In this manner, the film emphasizes the entitlement and ignorance of acknowledging the

Figure 2.6. The couple plans the attack in *The Second Bakery Attack*.

Figure 2.7. The couple robs the burger restaurant in *The Second Bakery Attack*.

exploitation of marginalized cultures around the world while at the same time victimizing ethnic minorities at home.

If ignoring the historical referentiality of the Bakery Attack series allows directors to move beyond an interpretive framework focused on radicalism in Japan, it also allows them to tease out other ways of reading the source texts. The time separating the production of the most recent adaptation of "The Second Bakery Attack"—Michal Wawrzecki's 2014 short film *Gorzko!* (*Bittersweet*)— from the original allows the film greater room for self-expression. Set in a completely different cultural context, contemporary Poland, Wawrzecki's film mutes the magical realist style that defamiliarizes postrevolutionary Japan in the source texts. Yet, this move away from Japan also allows the film to point back to Murakami's fiction to develop a theme often highlighted in his work—the incapacity to communicate with and understand other people. This theme is at the heart of Murakami's work going back to the beginning of his career. *Hear the Wind Sing* emphasizes the importance of communication, recalling the words of a psychiatrist to whom the narrator is sent by parents worried about his tendency toward reticence: "With civilization comes communication, he said. Whatever can't be expressed might as well not exist. Nothing."[18] The problems with communication that his characters experience as children extend to their adult relationships in novels like *The Wind-Up Bird Chronicle* (1994–1995). In that novel, the protagonist's wife, Kumiko, leaves home one day, leading him to question whether it is possible for him to completely understand her: "Is it possible, finally, for one human being to achieve perfect understanding of another? We can invest enormous time and energy in serious efforts to know another person, but in the end, how close are we able to come to that person's essence? We convince ourselves that we know the other person well, but do we really know anything important about anyone?"[19]

Resisting an interpretive framework based on postrevolutionary malaise, *Gorzko!* focuses on the relationship between the young newlywed couple—the prototype of future couples in Murakami's writing—and their challenge to get to know one another. Set on the day of their wedding, *Gorzko!* draws on the anxieties that many newlyweds experience having just committed their life to someone they do not know very well. Li Juan argues that the story highlights the uncertainty of marriage and how the creation of new rituals can serve to bind couples together.[20] The short film adapts the details in the original to examine these anxieties and how they are resolved through shared practices that dispel the ghosts of old relationships. Captured in a stylized fashion, the film opens with the couple greeting guests at their reception and then cuts to them sitting in their honeymoon suite complaining of hunger after the long day of wedding events. With little left to eat after the reception, the husband is reminded of the time he robbed a bakery and suggests that the two go out in search of an all-night diner. The wife is curious about the incident and why her husband never mentioned it before. This curiosity turns to jealousy when she learns that he carried out the robbery with a woman, a former girlfriend named Hanna (a plot point that deviates from the original story in which the protagonist's partner was a man). In this way, the motivation for the attack in *Gorzko!* is based in the bride's jealousy toward her husband's former lover and a desire to get to know him better, rather than in the historical trauma referenced in the original story.

As his wife drives the two of them through the dark streets in search of a diner, the husband relays the details of the robbery with Hanna. Flashbacks of the robbery are shown, creating a contrast between the husband's relationship with Hanna in the past and his relationship with his wife in the present day. From these scenes, we learn that the two would-be crooks, who appear to be on a drug bender (another real-world explanation for their actions), burst into a bakery and demanded bread from a startled baker. The scene then cuts to show the couple eating the bread while listening to music. Downplaying the socialist connotations of the exchange, the film focuses instead on the relationship between the newlyweds.

In an effort to exorcise the incident from their past, the woman suggests they rob another bakery together and grills her husband for details about the first attack so they can accurately replicate it. The groom gives in to her demands, because, as he suggests, "marriage is compromise." The two then head to the home of the bride's parents to get her father's gun before making their way to an all-night diner and demanding steak, fries, and beer, though, as with the Murakami story, they pay for the beers. They flee in their convertible, heading out into the country with the food, but instead of devouring the goods, they make love in the car, finally consummating their marriage. Though this version of the original source text is quite different from other films that draw on the significance of the activism that is alluded to in the originals, by focusing on the way the couple gets to know one another, *Gorzko!* nevertheless renews our reading of the story, drawing out a common Murakami theme that had been overshadowed by the focus on the disillusionment of failed activism in dominant interpretations of the story.

Perhaps more than other Murakami stories, the Bakery Attack series lends itself to adaptation in a variety of cultural contexts. Two stories about suburban crime have become a platform for raising issues about Marxist values, marital relationships, and the social conditions of different neoliberal economies in Asia

Figure 2.8. The robber's partner in the first bakery attack is a woman in *Gorzko.*

Figure 2.9. The couple bond after their robbery in *Gorzko*.

and around the world. Indeed, the greater the temporal and cultural distance from the original, the more these adaptations are able to resist the historical framework used to analyze the source texts since the films draw attention away from the intertextuality that exists between them in conventional readings. And yet, if the separation of time and distance allows films based on the series to tease out new meanings, it also revitalizes connections between author and original and the interpretive patterns used to understand the stories. In this way, the process of adaptation both develops the meaning of the stories as they travel around the world while at the same time reviving their connections to their origins.

# 3

# Unfaithful Adaptations
# in *Drive My Car*

Along with his status as a best-selling novelist, Murakami is known for his prolific career as a translator. Working over several decades, he has introduced some of the great works of modern American literature to a Japanese readership. His passion for American fiction, which he cultivated reading paperback translations as a youth in Kobe, inspired a career in translating over fifty works of literature by authors like Raymond Chandler, Truman Capote, F. Scott Fitzgerald, John Irving, and Tim O'Brien. And yet, for Murakami, writing stories and translating them into different languages are not separate endeavors; creating fiction involves an aspect of translation, while translating fictional works demands its own form of creative investment. Murakami shares, "My process of creative writing may closely correspond to the process of translation—or rather, in some respects they may be two sides of the same coin."[1] In fact, as is commonly known, Murakami's writing career began as a translation exercise. In an effort to forge a new literary style while working on *Hear the Wind Sing*, he famously wrote the first paragraph of the novel in English and then translated it into Japanese, seeking to preserve the syntactical flow of the original.

In addition to transporting meaning across languages, the idea of translation takes on other connotations in Murakami's work. Characters in his stories "translate" the often-complicated thoughts of one character for others. Amidst the overlapping ontologies in his works, characters carry meaning from one world to another, illuminating the dark underbelly of modern Japan by visiting its "other side."[2] Due to the various ways that Murakami and his novels translate, and are translated themselves, the very process of translation emerges as a main trope in cinematic adaptations of his stories. These adaptations do not just seek to render his literary imagination into another medium but also thematize how the translation process impacts his work in the first place. While this attention to translation references Murakami, creating ties between adaptations of his work and his own literary project, it also provides the means by which films based on his writing create distance from their source texts and take on a life of their own. Most recently, Hamaguchi Ryūsuke's 2021 adaptation of Murakami's short story "Drive My Car" examines the central function of translation in Murakami's work through its attention to the liberating effects of stories that travel from one medium to another—from literature to drama to cinema—and the way a connection to the original stories is solidified through both fidelity and infidelity to source texts in this process.

The film *Drive My Car* focuses on creative individuals who tell stories, perform them, and translate them for others. The work of these characters to craft narratives as actors, directors, and screenwriters self-consciously reflects the collaborative work of crafting *Drive My Car*. This collaborative work involves the authors who contributed to its source texts, including Hamaguchi, who wrote the screenplay for the film; Murakami, who is responsible for the stories on which the screenplay is based; and Anton Chekhov, who is the author of the story within the story, the play *Uncle Vanya*. Based primarily on Murakami's short story "Drive My Car" from his collection *Men without Women* (*Onna no inai otokotachi* [2014]), the story tells of Kafuku Yūsuke, a widowed actor who hires a twenty-four-year-old driver named Watari Misaki to chauffeur him around Tokyo in his yellow Saab. (Yūsuke is unable to drive due to a revoked license attributed to a drunk driving incident and the onset of glaucoma.) During their rides, Yūsuke tells Misaki about his career as an actor and about his late wife's many affairs. He tells of his relationship with one of his wife's lovers, a young stage actor named Takatsuki Kōji, whom he initially befriends with the intention of undermining but instead learns to confide in as the two regularly meet up for drinks at bars around Tokyo. Yet, even as he develops a relationship with Kōji, his inability to grasp his wife's motives for betraying him creates a "blind spot" in his understanding of her.

Hamaguchi's adaptation fleshes out Yūsuke's relationship with his wife and Misaki's backstory while altering some details from the source material. In fact, the first forty minutes of the film, before the opening credits play, provide context for the original source text. In the film, Yūsuke is a theater actor and director who is married to a screenplay writer named Oto (the Japanese word for "sound"). The two share a close relationship that is based on the theatrical nature of their jobs. Oto comes up with the plots for her scripts during intimate moments with Yūsuke, and she records dialogue to help him practice lines for plays in which he performs. However, as close as they are as a couple, there is a side of Oto that Yūsuke is unable to access. To his dismay, Yūsuke learns that Oto conducts affairs with other men, including a young actor named Takatsuki Kōji. After this revelation comes to light, Oto suddenly passes away from a brain hemorrhage one evening, before she is able to confess these affairs to her husband.

At this point, the film skips ahead two years to find Yūsuke driving from Tokyo to Hiroshima to direct a multilingual stage play based on Chekhov's *Uncle Vanya* for a performing arts center in the city. We see his Saab—red in the film version—driving on the outskirts of Hiroshima as the credits role. Once he gets to Hiroshima, he learns that the troupe has hired a young woman named Watari Misaki as his chauffeur due to insurance requirements. While Misaki drives him around town in his Saab, Yūsuke listens to recordings of Oto's lines from *Uncle Vanya*. (Throughout most of the film, Oto manifests as a disembodied voice channeled through these recordings.) As in the original story, Yūsuke begins to confide his feelings to Misaki about his wife's infidelities. Meanwhile, as the troupe prepares the performance, Yūsuke auditions several actors, including Takatsuki, whom he casts in the title role, a part that Yūsuke himself played in earlier performances. Through the relationship he develops with Misaki and Takatsuki, Yūsuke seeks to reconcile his love for Oto with the side of her that continues to elude him.

Though the film takes its name from "Drive My Car," it also borrows narrative elements from two other stories from *Men without Women*: "Scheherazade" and "Kino." "Scheherazade" tells of man named Habara, a thirty-one-year-old shut-in who is regularly treated in his home by a female nurse he names Scheherazade. After each visit, Scheherazade entertains Habara with stories, including one in which she details regular visits to her boyfriend's home when he is not there to leave a "token" behind in his room—the same story that Oto begins to tell Yūsuke in *Drive My Car* before she dies. From the story "Kino," *Drive My Car* borrows a scenario involving a young husband, like Yūsuke, who buries his pain when he discovers his wife's affairs. (The reason Yūsuke comes home late in the film is to avoid talking about this issue with his wife, much like the main character in "Kino.")[3] Hamaguchi explains his reason for combining elements from these three different stories in making the film:

> ["Drive My Car"] itself is only about 40 pages long, so I didn't think that there was enough material to create a film. I had to bring other elements from two other stories in the same Haruki Murakami collection [*Men without Women*]. One is "Scheherazade" and the other is "Kino." In the text, the "Drive My Car" story starts after the death of the wife, but for the movie I needed to portray the past and also the future. To depict the past and the character of the wife, I took the story from "Scheherazade," which is the story of a woman who tells a story after having sex. The other story, "Kino," was used to portray the future that was not part of the original

"Drive My Car" story. In "Kino," the main character is a husband whose wife has an affair. Towards the end of the story this husband realizes that he should have faced his wife in a more proper manner.[4]

From these source texts, Hamaguchi creates a film that thematizes acts of storytelling, translation, and adaptation as a means of communication and as a way to uncover the truth about human relationships. Indeed, as Aaron Gerow argues, Hamaguchi combines Murakami's stories to effectively write a new story that sheds light on the meaning of the originals.[5] One of the main points of conflict in the film is a breakdown in communication between storyteller and listener. Murakami has explored this theme from the beginning of his career, as discussed in the previous chapter, and deals with it in *Drive My Car* through the relationship between Yūsuke and Oto. Oto's premature death leaves Yūsuke without closure regarding the reason for her infidelity. Yūsuke admits to Takatsuki that Oto contained within her "a spot that I couldn't access, where darkness swirled." In response, Kōji acknowledges the impossibility of ever fully knowing someone: "No matter how much you love someone, or think you know them, you can't completely see into their heart."

Overcoming the wall separating speaker and listener requires acts of translation, a term which is treated broadly in the film, manifesting through the rendering of written scripts from one language to another, the interpretation of spoken dialogue, and even the process of adapting from one artistic medium to another. The central function translation plays in the story is underscored through the multilingual nature of the dialogue in the film, an artistic choice that seemingly impedes communication by creating more barriers between speaker and listener. To stage Yūsuke's version of *Uncle Vanya*, the troupe auditions actors from several different linguistic backgrounds. Together with his assistant—a Korean national named Gong Yoon-soo, who speaks Japanese—Yūsuke casts Japanese speakers, a native Chinese speaker who also understands English (Janice Chang), and a Korean mute woman (Lee Yoo-na), who is married to Yoon-soo and who communicates through sign language but can also understand spoken Korean. The different languages used on set necessitate acts of translation and interpretation in rehearsals. Yūsuke gives instructions to the cast in Japanese and English. To communicate with Yoo-na, he speaks in Japanese while Yoon-soo translates his words into spoken Korean and also interprets Yoo-na's sign language. During the performances, each cast member speaks in their native tongue while translations of their lines are projected above the stage in Japanese and English. That the characters often do not understand each other requires them to "go by feeling" when performing dialogue, as Hamaguchi explains: "Listening focuses on comprehending the voice, but things are also communicated through body language. By using all of these different languages, it was almost like I was letting the meaning be expressed through the body more. Sign language was another step in that direction. It's a more direct form of communication in terms of body movement and expression. And it's a beautiful medium of communication."[6]

Another form of translation that occurs in the film is adaptation: the transference of meaning across artistic mediums, from the formal language of literature to the language of theater and cinema. Adaptation critic Patrick Cattrysse accentuates the similarities between translation and adaptation, suggesting the notion of translation should not be reduced to "interlinguistic relationships only" but should extend to relate to other "semiotic" acts like cinematic adaptation.[7] Cynthia Tsui, likewise, argues that "adaptation and translation share a similar set of debates," including "fidelity vs. creativity, author vs. adaptor/translator," etc.[8] Accordingly, adaptation as a form of translation, the film suggests, necessitates faithfulness to the original material in order to communicate its meaning or effect. Fidelity to source texts is a point of concern for Yūsuke in his adaptation of *Uncle Vanya* as a multilingual production. The second part of *Drive My Car* primarily tells the story of directing *Uncle Vanya*, a play that depicts the visit of a married couple—a professor and his young wife—to their estate in the countryside. The titular character, Vanya, who is the brother of the husband's late wife, manages the estate. During their stay at the estate, the young wife, Yelena, catches the eyes of Vanya and a local doctor named Astrov. At the same time, the professor's daughter, Sonya, who works with her uncle, Vanya, on the estate, develops feelings for Astrov. The love triangle tensions come to a head once the professor declares that he plans to sell the estate. (The emotional tension created by this story within a story reflects the tension in *Drive My Car*, created by the betrayals and jealousies that arise from infidelity.) Yūsuke's desire to be faithful to the play is evident in the care he takes in rehearsal to honor the original. For the first few weeks of preparation, he conducts table reads of the source text with the cast, instructing them to deliver the dialogue slowly and carefully without emotional inflection, avoiding interpretation. He reassures the cast that they do not need to perform the script to a certain standard but rather just "yield themselves to the text." The process of preparing for the theatrical production in the film resembles the same process that Hamaguchi uses in creating his films, as the director suggests:

> Indeed, much of the film's image of the rehearsals responds to my methods. With some exceptions because, after all, the film needs drama. I do focus on repetitions of reading the script without emotions included in it. We go through the text over and over again until the words become embedded in the actors' bodies and they can deliver the lines automatically. I want my actors to get rid of their expectations towards the characters but also avoid any clichés. It's all about nuances. Once the actors get on that level and the words blend with the body, the ability to

Figure 3.1. The drama troupe conducts table reads in *Drive My Car*.

Figure 3.2. Watari chauffeurs Kōji in *Drive My Car*.

deliver can spread in different directions. They become more focused; but above all, the process of opening up puts them at ease. And that is the most effective way to work with actors. To act while being relaxed.[9]

Yet if acts of translation honor texts and the limits of the medium through which they are relayed, they also acknowledge the way creative infidelity can enhance the meaning of the original for the audience, allowing them to see it in a new way. As Murakami's writing demonstrates, stories can often develop beyond their original limits because the process of translating into another language or form reveals the stories' intertextual nature and the layers of mediation that come between them and the translation. For instance, Lee Chang-dong's 2018 film, *Burning* (which will be discussed in the next chapter), an adaptation of Murakami's "Barn Burning," does not treat the original Murakami story as a hermeneutically sealed work but rather acknowledges the network of intertextuality built into the story by drawing attention to other literary allusions in its subtext. While *Burning* unearths references to Faulkner's "Barn Burning" in Murakami's version by repeating similar plot details, it also goes beyond Faulkner to excavate other intertexts, such as F. Scott Fitzgerald's 1925 novel, *The Great Gatsby*, a book that Murakami himself translated into Japanese. In *Burning*, Lee evokes *The Great Gatsby* through the character Ben, whom the protagonist relates to Gatsby: "[He is] a mysterious person who is young and rich," and yet "you don't know what [he] really [does]." Though Faulkner provides the most obvious literary referent for *Burning*, Lee's adaptation releases the narrative from this single source text, teasing out other allusions by viewing the film in relation to Murakami's own work as a translator.

Having translated many works, Murakami recognizes the capacity for translations and adaptations to expand and develop the meaning of his own fiction. Murakami mentions that he enjoys reading translations of his stories as autonomous works rather than as second-rate copies because their distance from him allows these translations to illuminate other aspects of his writing:

> For me, one of the joys of my works being translated into another language is that I can reread them in a new form. By having a work converted into another language by someone else's hand, I can look back and reconsider it from a respectable distance and enjoy it coolly as a quasi-outsider, as it were, whereas I never would have read it again if it had remained only in Japanese. . . . Put differently, when a literary world that I have created is transposed into another linguistic system, I feel as if I have been able to dissociate me from myself, which gives me a good deal of peace.[10]

In fact, Murakami enjoyed Alfred Birnbaum's English translation of his novels so much that he tried to reproduce Birnbaum's unique style as he penned subsequent works in Japanese, highlighting the fluidity that exists between the roles of author and translator.[11] Chikako Nihei suggests that Murakami's experiences in gaining insight from the way translations produce a new way of representing his stories may even "encourage translators to carry out language experiments of their own, taking initiatives and making individual choices" in how they render Murakami's work into different languages.[12] This is perhaps why Murakami keeps his distance from the production of cinematic adaptations of his writing, which he considers to be a product of the creative work of directors.[13] Hamaguchi comments on Murakami's hands-off approach in the production of *Drive My Car*: "We got permission from [Murakami], but we had very little contact. Every time I did a rewrite of the script, I'd send it to him, but there was no feedback. We invited him to a screening, but he didn't come. So I thought, 'Maybe he's not interested in this movie.' But I learned that he did watch the movie at his local movie theater with his wife. I heard that he enjoyed it through a New York Times article."[14]

Notwithstanding Murakami's ambivalence toward films based on his work, the thematic focus on translation in *Drive My Car* references his literary persona as author and translator while providing the mechanism by which the film develops the meaning of the source text. The process of adapting Chekhov's play into a multilingual version activates the creative potential of both fidelity and infidelity. The close attention the actors give to the original story, and its framing through the scripted performances that occur within the circumscribed space of the stage, reinforces the limits of the source text. Yet, the creative license Yūsuke and Hamaguchi take in adapting the original into a multilingual format also generates meaning, allowing it to provide new perspectives on the story. Yūsuke's and Hamaguchi's adaptations flesh out the meaning of the play *Uncle Vanya*, which is treated superficially in "Drive My Car," as the story details Yūsuke's daily routine: "Yūsuke practiced his lines on the way, reciting with the cassette recording. The play was a Meiji-era adaptation of Chekhov's Uncle Vanya. He played the role of Uncle Vanya. He knew the lines by heart, but ran through them anyway to calm his nerves before a performance. This was his long-standing habit."[15]

In Hamaguchi's film, on the other hand, Chekhov's play becomes central to the story as it is adapted for stage and film. By virtue of the capacity of film to move beyond the bounded space of the stage, Hamaguchi is able to use Chekhov's words to introduce new layers to the story, a reflection of the way *Drive My Car* develops the impact of its source text. Although the perspective of the viewer is bounded or confined in theater, due to the fixed position from which they view the performance and the limited space provided by the stage on which this performance occurs, film liberates the viewer's perspective to a certain degree by moving away from the stage and capturing a variety of perspectives on dramatic events through a camera apparatus that can move about more freely within the diegetic world. Performances of *Uncle Vanya* at various points in the film are shot to recreate the front-on perspective of audience members watching a stage play, thus merging the perspective of theater and film while also utilizing the capacity of moving cameras to surpass the 180 degrees allowed by theater and capture 360 degrees of space. Throughout the film, the representational capacity of a mobile viewing apparatus brushes up against the limits of the theatrical form, periodically moving beyond them to flesh out characters and their relationships. To rehearse

Figure 3.3. Yoo-na and Janice rehearse a scene while
the troupe watches in *Drive My Car*.

Figure 3.4. The camera captures the nuances of Yoo-na and
Janice's performance in *Drive My Car*.

the play, the troupe heads to a park on a warm day after completing a few weeks of
table reads. Finding a space on some benches that form the circular outlines of a
stage, Yūsuke asks Yoo-na and Janice to perform a scene for the rest of the troupe.
Standing in front of the group as if on a stage, the two deliver their lines while the
camera captures their performance from behind the audience members, who sit in
a semicircle around them. Though the camera can directly capture the perspective

created by the stage, its capacity to reposition the viewing perspective reveals the nuances of their performance. The limitations of the theatrical setting become apparent as improvisational blocking moves actors around the stage, requiring the camera to pan to keep them within the frame. To better capture the fluid interaction between the actors, the camera jumps back and forth across the axis line, creating a series of shot-reverse shots that expand the viewer's perspective beyond that of the other actors in the troupe. In shots when the camera is positioned on the other side of the axis line, it places Janice and Yoo-na in the foreground and the rest of the actors in the background, reversing the original blocking. As the two actors embrace during one part of their performance, Janice whispers lines in Yoo-na's ear far from the listening range of the group. The two actors share an intimate moment, exchanging smiles that only the viewer of the film, not the built-in audience, can see. At this point, the scene has transformed from a theatrical moment to a cinematic one; its meaning is expanded through the intervention of a mobile camera that provides enhanced access to performances, fleshing out the meaning of the source text and its presentation on stage.

Camera movement, furthermore, develops the meaning of the Chekhov drama as well as the emotional experience of the characters who perform the play in *Drive My Car*. By virtue of its unrestrained movement, the camera captures how the real and the fictional merge during the performances of *Uncle Vanya* that occur after Oto's death and at the end of the film. Cutting straight from Oto's funeral to the stage, the scene opens on a shot of Yūsuke playing the titular role of *Uncle Vanya* in Tokyo, allowing the viewer to see the audience's viewing of it. And yet, the viewer can also see what the audience of the play cannot. As Yūsuke turns away from the audience and faces the camera, the viewer catches a moment of hesitancy in his performance. As he turns to face the crowd and deliver his lines, the camera jumps the axis line to set up on the right side. As the dialogue builds to a climax, Yūsuke walks offstage to retrieve a gun that he will use to shoot another character (a subtle nod to the "Chekhov's gun" principle of narrative economy). The camera cuts to where the gun is stored offstage. The viewer sees Yūsuke approach the firearm only to pause, unable to continue on, emotionally compromised by both his wife's sudden passing as well as his feelings of betrayal, something that the love-triangle structure of the play *Uncle Vanya* in which he is performing brings to the surface.

Yet, the camera cannot stray too far from the stage, just as the adaptation cannot deviate too much from the source text. Along with restoring balance to the characters' relationships, *Drive My Car* seeks to harmonize the connection between film and stage, and between adaptation and source text. In the final performance of *Uncle Vanya* in Hiroshima, the unbounding impulse of the camera and the boundedness of the stage work in collaboration with one another. During the

Figure 3.5. The camera captures Yūsuke break down off stage in *Drive My Car*.

Figure 3.6. The camera captures the action on stage from the
perspective of the audience in *Drive My Car*.

performance, the camera captures the drama from a variety of perspectives: from
that of audience members, suggesting the limits of the theatrical performance,
and from other perspectives that allow a multidimensional viewing offered by
film. These perspectives include shots from behind and even offstage as the actors
prepare for their scenes in a break room, where they watch the play on a monitor
relaying a closed broadcast.

With the help of this moving camera, we see Yūsuke's development throughout the film, as he takes over the part of Vanya from Kōji, who drops out of the play at the end. Repeating the same scene that he struggled to complete in his Tokyo performance, Yūsuke once again walks offstage to retrieve the pistol for the pivotal moment. Pausing to catch his breath, Yūsuke avoids an emotional breakdown and returns to the stage to carry out the scene (finally shooting the gun that was foreshadowed at the start of the film), while the camera captures all the action that occurs offstage, giving us greater insight into Yūsuke's narrative arc. Yet, notwithstanding the expanded view provided by the cinematic apparatus, the camera yields to the stage in the final scene of the play, which is fittingly shot front-on from a traditional theatrical perspective and captures Yoo-na standing behind Yūsuke as the two perform the final act of Chekhov's play. In this way, *Drive My Car* suggests that harmonizing the creative potential of fidelity and infidelity in the cinematic depiction of the original is essential in truly understanding the layers of the source text and the relationships it seeks to portray.

Creative forms of adaptation also allow stories to shed light on historical and cultural contexts beyond those intended by the original text. Reworking the meaning of Murakami's stories through adaptation reveals thematic links that naturally form between his stories. Though not a part of the original Murakami story, the trip that Misaki and Yūsuke take to northern Japan at the end of the film draws attention to the aftermath of the 2011 Tōhoku earthquake and tsunami. This natural disaster is conflated in adaptations based on Murakami's writing about another disaster, the Great Hanshin Earthquake Disaster of 1995, which Murakami treats in his short story collection *After the Quake*.

Adaptation also connects the cultural experiences of Murakami's characters with those in other traditions, demonstrating the global influence of his work. This connection occurs in the feature film *All God's Children Can Dance* by Robert Logevall, which is based on the Murakami short story by the same name (published in English in *After the Quake* [2002]). Many of the stories in the collection deal with the Tokyo subway gas attacks of 1995 perpetrated by the fringe religious group Aum Supreme Truth (Aum Shinrikyō), which killed thirteen passengers and injured many more. In response to the attack, many stories in *After the Quake* deal with the seductiveness of Aum's religious views that inspired normal Japanese people to join the group and commit acts of terrorism. Murakami's "All God's Children Can Dance" tells of a young man named Yoshiya who lives with his single-parent mother, an avid Christian evangelical, who takes Yoshiya with her on door-to-door proselyting missions. Yoshiya's mother told him from a young age that he is the son of God, but he suspects that his father is a doctor who treated his mother. Logevall's adaptation, *All God's Children Can Dance*, translates the experience of religious fervor for a world audience. The film is true to the original, including the same characters and general plot line, but it changes the characters' names. The one major difference from the original is that the film is set in Koreatown in Los Angeles, one of the centers of Christianity among the Korean American population in California. Certainly, the story plays on the angst of growing up in a community steeped in religious practice and resonates with audiences who grew up in this type of environment.

While the layered treatment of literature, theater, and film in *Drive My Car* seemingly interferes with the film's communicative capacities, these layers actually work to enhance the film's ability to relay meaning. The limited extent to which we can recover original meaning from a novel or film is likened to the limited extent to which we can really know another person, a common theme in Murakami's writing. In addressing the way meaning is dispersed or obfuscated in artistic meaning and interpersonal relationships, *Drive My Car* does not seek to cut through the layered meanings within communication but embrace them, suggesting that accentuating mediation actually enhances the film's communicative capacities by allowing for the recovery of a multidimensional perspective on experience. Because the characters avoid directly referencing an original source, the linguistic and cinematic layers that come between characters are the very means by which a balance between faithfulness to the original and the creative function of adaptation is maintained. Themes of fidelity and infidelity manifest throughout *Drive My Car*, perfectly personified in Misaki and Oto through their degree of faithfulness to Yūsuke and even in their driving styles. Misaki's close attention to traffic regulations when she drives Yūsuke's red Saab reflects the impulse toward fidelity to the original while Oto's inability to stay within the lines embodies a creative impulse to push against boundaries.

This mediating function built into *Drive My Car* is carried out by two types of characters (the storyteller and the double) who appear throughout Murakami's work. Storytellers in Murakami's fiction do not simply play a supporting role in a larger story; they assume narrative duties themselves. These characters process their own history and identity through long tales they share in letters or conversations. The emphasis on storytelling as a means of understanding oneself and communicating this self to others is apparent in *The Wind-Up Bird Chronicle* (1994–1995). For example, the scarred war veteran Lt. Mamiya relays the horrors he experienced during World War II to the narrator through letters, which occupy several chapters in the novel. Likewise, Cinnamon, the silent son of an enigmatic businesswoman, comes to understand the meaning of his existence by combining stories about his grandfather, handed down to him from his mother, with his own experience:

> But why, finally, had Cinnamon written such stories? And why stories? Why not some other form? And why had he found it necessary to use the word chronicle in the title? I thought about these things while seated

on the fitting room sofa, turning a colored design pencil over and over in my hand. I probably would have had to read all sixteen stories to find the answers to my questions, but even after a single reading of #8, I had some idea, however vague, of what Cinnamon was looking for in his writing. He was engaged in a serious search for the meaning of his own existence. And he was hoping to find it by looking into the events that had preceded his birth. To do that, Cinnamon had to fill in those blank spots in the past that he could not reach with his own hands. By using those hands to make a story, he was trying to supply the missing links. From the stories he had heard repeatedly from his mother, he derived further stories in an attempt to re-create the enigmatic figure of his grandfather in a new setting.[16]

Often, storytelling becomes a collaborative experience in Murakami's writing, as characters benefit from a sounding board to help them sort through their experiences. Storytellers serve an ethical role in Murakami's fiction, Rebecca Suter argues, by acting as conduits through which "hidden sides of characters and realities surface and enter 'this world.'"[17] The character Naoko from *Norwegian Wood* (1987) struggles to express herself through words, relying on the listening ear of the narrator, who helps her process her experiences. The narrator relates the following:

> Naoko was unusually talkative that night. She told me about her childhood, her school, her family. Each episode was a long one, executed with the painstaking detail of a miniature. I was amazed at the power of her memory, but as I sat listening it began to dawn on me that there was something wrong with the way she was telling these stories: something strange, warped even. Each tale had its own internal logic, but the link from one to the next was odd. Before you knew it, story A had turned into story B, which had been contained in A, and then came C from something in B, with no end in sight.[18]

To prevent the relationship between storytellers and characters from stagnating—and to keep storytellers from seizing control over the narrative function of others—like K in *Sputnik Sweetheart* (1999)—Murakami deliberately imposes mediation into the storytelling process by making it a combined exercise between three characters. (His novels, Murakami claims, are based on a triangular conversation between characters, like Toru, Naoko, and Reiko in *Norwegian Wood*, and K, Sumire, and Miu in *Sputnik Sweetheart*.)[19] These relationships, which often manifest as love triangles, form blockages or blind spots that forestall resolution, as is the case with the unusual relationship between K, Sumire, and Miu discussed in the first chapter.

Yet, while keeping storytellers from controlling others, triangular relationships also enhance communication between characters by allowing for different perspectives to emerge. Okamuro Minako argues that characters in *Drive My Car* serve as intermediaries of other voices.[20] The mediating function of characters in the film is shown most clearly in the relationship between Yūsuke, Oto, and Kōji. While both Yūsuke and Kōji love Oto, neither of them can have her completely: Yūsuke has Oto's devotion but lacks her fidelity. Kōji enjoys a sexual relationship with her but lacks the devotion she gives only to Yūsuke. Throughout the film, Yūsuke's blind spot, his lack of understanding about his wife's motives, prevents him from moving on after her death. At the same time, the very workings of triangular desire that frustrate his efforts to understand his wife also help him find closure at the end of the film.

The closure that Yūsuke seeks in his relationship with Oto is realized in the resolution provided by the story she began to tell him before her death. It is a story that all three characters collaborate in telling. Initially, Oto forgets the details of the story as she relays them to Yūsuke one night, depending on her husband to relay them back to her the next morning. Thinking Oto died without completing her story, Yūsuke is surprised to learn that she told the conclusion to Kōji, who in turn relays it back to Yūsuke as the two ride in the back seat of his Saab. Depicted in shot-reverse shots with Yūsuke, Kōji is shot front-on, making it impossible to look away from him as he completes the story for Yūsuke. Yet, even as he holds the key to Oto's unfinished tale, Kōji also admits that he lacks even a fraction of the understanding of Oto that Yūsuke possesses, confessing his outsider status. Because each character fills in gaps created by the blind spots of the other members of the triangular configuration, all three characters must contribute in some way in order for Yūsuke to find closure in his and Oto's relationship. In this way, the layers of mediation that come between characters—just like the layers of signification that come between the actors performing *Uncle Vanya* on stage— allow them to unearth meaning that is only accessible through their displacement from the center of the storytelling process by means of the mediating function of other characters.

Along with triangular relationships, *Drive My Car* incorporates Murakami's use of literary doppelgängers (doubles) to flesh out the different sides of its main characters. The notion of the double easily translates into cinematic representation because of its image-oriented nature. Doubles in Murakami's fiction act like negatives in photography; they offer a contrasting view of the image, revealing the parts it does not show. Doubling through mirrors serves as a central motif in the film. Yūsuke sees his wife having sex with another man—presumably Kōji, though his face is obscured—through a giant mirror in their living room upon walking through the door of their apartment. Later, Oto and Yūsuke have sex on

Figure 3.7. Kōji is shot front on as he talks with Yūsuke
in the back of his red Saab in *Drive My Car*.

Figure 3.8. Oto is introduced as a silhouette in *Drive My Car*.

the same couch, creating a mirror image of the previous incident. Moreover, since she passed away early, Oto haunts Yūsuke through various doubles that appear in the film. These appearances demonstrate the way he comes to understand the different sides of his wife concealed by the blind spot in his awareness of her. In the first shot of the film, Oto is introduced to the viewer as sound attached to the silhouette of a woman, a disembodiment that allows her to settle into two

Figure 3.9. Yoo-na in *Drive My Car*.

Figure 3.10. Yoo-na embraces Yūsuke from behind in *Drive My Car*.

embodied forms—Yoo-na and Misaki—which eventually manifest the parts of Oto to which Yūsuke lacked access. Through Yoo-na, the film provides the negative image of Oto, who has a physical body but is silent. The film opens with just Oto's voice and the silhouette of her body as she narrates the story to Yūsuke and ends with the opposite, a view of Yoo-na silently signing lines to Yūsuke while embracing him from behind.

Furthermore, like Yoo-na, Misaki fills out Yūsuke's understanding of Oto. Similar to the stage on which Yoo-na performs, the interior of the red Saab serves as both real space—where true feelings are expressed—and a stage on which lines are delivered and performances occur, allowing Misaki to take on the role of double for Oto. The interior of the car, Hamaguchi explains, came to serve as a central idea in the film: "I was attracted to the relationship between Yūsuke and Watari and their conversations taking place inside the car. I thought it was interesting that the relationship develops in that very enclosed space."[21] It is in this space that Yūsuke gets in touch with his wife by connecting to her opposite. The laconic Misaki is a good driver, always staying within the lines, while Oto, who talks all the time, constantly strays from her lane, which Yūsuke complains about early in the film. Like Oto, Misaki drives Yūsuke through the city streets, and long shots of the car with the sound of Oto reading lines makes it sound as if Oto is driving. Inside the car, as Oto's voice plays, Misaki is framed in a way that suggests she is speaking Oto's lines.

As doubles of Oto, Yoo-na and Misaki illuminate the blind spot in Yūsuke's understanding of his wife. While embracing Yūsuke from behind during their performance of *Uncle Vanya* at the end of the film, Yoo-na encourages Yūsuke, through Chekhov's lines, to endure the trauma and grief he experienced after her death, words of comfort that he was waiting to hear from Oto. Similarly, Misaki helps resolve Yūsuke's confusion and pain concerning Oto's betrayals as she accompanies him on a trip to her home in Hokkaido, suggesting that Oto's need to sleep with other men does not diminish her love for Yūsuke.[22]

Because the possibility of communicating across mediums like stories, letters, and conversations is a central theme in Murakami's work, it is natural that this theme carries over in cinematic adaptations of his work. For Murakami, translation is not just a process that is required of him as an author with global appeal; it is also a central part of the ethics of his literary project. For Murakami, communication does not just require the capacity to relay stories to others, as many of his characters do; it also requires the capacity to adapt them so that they can be understood.

# 4

# Merging Matter and Memory in *Norwegian Wood, Tony Takitani,* and *Burning*[1]

Recent cinematic adaptations of Murakami Haruki's fiction visualize a central theme in his work: the division in Japan's historical imagination between its tumultuous past and its contemporary postindustrial consumer culture. The adaptations *Tony Takitani* (2004), by Ichikawa Jun, and *Norwegian Wood* (2010), by Trần Anh Hùng, depict how the memory of war, recovery, and activism come to bear on the experience of rapid development in Japan. However, based on the popularity of Murakami's fiction in the larger region of East Asia, the impact of modernization on cultural memory is a theme that does not just resonate with audiences in Japan. South Korean director Lee Chang-dong's film *Burning* (2018), based on Murakami's "Barn Burning," depicts the fractures formed between South Korea's hypermodern present and the cultural experiences that were suppressed in the nation's rapid development. Much like adaptations of Murakami's fiction set in Japan, *Burning* upsets the self-evidence of the highly developed condition of present-day South Korea by making the material experience of an affluent Seoul landscape somehow less real while giving tangible form instead to the virtual effects of the nation's divisive history. The melding of the virtual dimensions of the past with the materiality of the present in Murakami adaptations set in both Japan and South Korea suggests a similar experience with the illusory nature of rapid development in the historical imagination of both these national traditions.

A central theme in Murakami's fiction is the impact of the past on present experience. The novels *Norwegian Wood* (1987); *South of the Border, West of the Sun* (1992); *Sputnik Sweetheart* (1999); *Kafka on the Shore* (2005); and *1Q84* (2011), among others, deal with the way fragments of memory, nostalgia, and history impact the here and now. Often, critics working on the construction of national and regional history in Murakami's fiction seek to define the historical past as "other" to the reality of the present. Nathan Clerici argues that Murakami uses a form of "false history" as a reflection of changing consumption patterns in the 1980s.[2] Jiwoon Baik, moreover, argues that the past in Murakami's work manifests as an "abstract and universal nostalgia, which is closed to the present."[3] And yet, suggesting that personal and collective forms of history in Murakami's work are "closed off" from the here and now risks privileging the living present as a stable and self-evident counterbalance to an elusive and inaccessible past. As the cinematic adaptations of Murakami's work explored in this chapter suggest, the interrelationship between the historical past and present in Murakami's vision of contemporary Japan becomes apparent when his fiction is translated into an artistic medium based in the representation of time.

The openness of the present to the past in Murakami's fictional worlds is accentuated through the temporal dimensions of the cinematic adaptations of his work. As film critics suggest, the cinematic medium finds its aesthetic foundations in the experience of time. If language is the basis of literature, Russian filmmaker Andrei Tarkovsky argues, time serves as the "base of all bases" for cinema.[4] Perhaps more than any other theorist, Gilles Deleuze considers the temporal experience of cinema in his work—particularly, *Cinema 2* (1989)—in which he builds on critic Henri Bergson's early work on temporality and filmic representation. In *Matter and Memory* (1896), Bergson challenges the rigid identification of memory with the past and "matter" (physical experience) with the present, suggesting a much more permeable boundary existing between the two: "In real time, in the life of consciousness, our self is at every moment . . . absorbing its past and creating its future."[5] According to Bergson, the past, in the form of memory, merges with matter in the present: "While time eclipses the matter of the previous moment, it is in the present that consciousness, as memory, meets matter, transforming it from the latter to the former."[6] In this way, the present moment is not cut off from the past for Bergson but rather serves as the location where they meet: "The fluidity and continuity of time implies that the past . . . is always present, merging its materiality with that of the present moment."[7]

Deleuze develops Bergson's work on the temporality of film, a medium, he argues, that allows viewers to see this complex flow of time. In *Cinema 2*, he differentiates between the presentation of time in conventional forms of film like classical Hollywood cinema, which subordinates temporal experience to the purposes of narrative development, and the presentation of what he calls the "time image," or a direct view of the passing of time itself.[8] In contrast to a linear model of time, Deleuze identifies a more dynamic interaction between past, present, and future in the time image. Time figures "as the power of difference or becoming whereby we move from . . . all of the possible creations and tendencies"—what Deleuze calls the "virtual"—to the actual development of lived experience.[9] In the time image, time does not move between discrete events that constitute the past, present, and future. Just as a memory interrupts the flow of everyday life, Deleuze suggests, the virtual past invades the actual present rather than serving as a static point against which it gains meaning.

The confluence of memory and matter occurs in what Deleuze describes as "time crystals," moments within which the virtual states of the past transform into the actual experience of the present. Deleuze uses the idea of a time crystal as a metaphor for the way audiences experience the reciprocal exchange between the actual and virtual in cinematic images. In time crystals, the transformation from past to present does not occur through a linear process but through moments of convergence in which the difference between the two is rendered imperceptible.[10] In this process, Deleuze argues, the virtual takes on properties of the actual, and vice versa, until memory gives way to matter and actual experience: "Time in the crystal is differentiated into two movements, but one of the two takes charge of the future and freedom, on condition that it leave the crystal. Thus, the future will be created at the same time that it escapes the eternal recurrence of the actual and virtual, of the present and the past."[11]

Filmic adaptations of Murakami's stories visualize this reciprocity between the materiality of actual experience and the virtual dimensions of memory—a reciprocity that is also depicted in his fiction.[12] Scholarship on Murakami identifies the manifestation of crystals like these as portals or entrances to different realms. Matthew Strecher recognizes several such portals in Murakami's work: "Over time Murakami has expanded his repertoire of such passageways to include elevator shafts, telephone lines, hallways, subway tunnels, ladders, sewers, and subterranean caves, among other things."[13] The other world that lies on the other side of these portals, Strecher suggests, has developed from an ambiguous realm to a place of its own:

> There is, of course, no one simple way of describing the "other world," given the guises it takes across the broad spectrum of the author's repertoire, a fact that has contributed, no doubt, to the variety of labels that have been applied to it. I have generally preferred terms such as metaphysical realm and other world, but many Japanese critics opt for the even less specific *achiragawa*, or "over there." Part of our challenge lies in the fact that this *achiragawa* is many things at once: a metaphysical zone, freed from the constraints of time and space; a wormhole, or conduit into other physical worlds; an unconscious shared space, similar to Jung's collective unconscious; a repository for memories, dreams, and visions; the land of the dead; the "world soul" of mysticism; heaven or hell; eternity.[14]

However, what adaptations of Murakami's fiction have taught readers is that these portals do not just raise ontological issues but temporal ones as well; they help readers envision these entryways not just as dividers between different worlds but also time periods. Trần's *Norwegian Wood* envisions the melding of the virtual and physical that occurs in the workings of memory. Its source material, the novel *Norwegian Wood* published in 1987, created a phenomenon in Japan by achieving record sales of over four million copies. This success led to popularity in Asia and the rest of the world, as translations went on sale in Taiwan, South Korea, Hong Kong, Shanghai, and, eventually, the United States and Europe. Set against the larger backdrop of student activism during the 1960s in Japan, a period Murakami experienced firsthand, the novel is told in flashback by Toru. Many years after the events of the story, he recalls his college days when he hears the Beatles' ballad playing on the intercom on a flight to Germany. The song acts as a time crystal that fuses his experience in the present with the memory of his youth:

> The plane reached the gate. People began unlatching their seatbelts and pulling baggage from the storage bins, and all the while I was in the meadow. I could smell the grass, feel the wind on my face, hear the cries of the birds. Autumn 1969, and soon I would be twenty. The stewardess came to check on me again. This time she sat next to me and asked if I was all right. . . . Eighteen years have gone by, and still I can bring back every detail of that day in the meadow. Washed clean of summer's dust by days of gentle rain, the mountains wore a deep, brilliant green. The October breeze set white fronds of head-tall grasses swaying. One long streak of cloud hung pasted across a dome of frozen blue. It almost hurt to look at that far off sky. A puff of wind swept across the meadow and through her hair before it slipped into the woods to rustle branches and send back snatches of distant barking—a hazy sound that seemed to reach us from the doorway to another world. We heard no other sounds. We met no other people. We saw only two bright, red birds leap startled from the center of the meadow and dart into the woods. As we ambled along, Naoko spoke to me of wells.[15]

The film *Norwegian Wood* establishes a difference between past and present through its development of characters who embody a temporal division associated with linear time. It jumps between Toru's experiences with Naoko and Midori. Naoko is a figment of the past; she is the girlfriend of Toru's best friend in college, Kizuki, whose suicide has a lasting effect on her emotional well-being. Like the past, she is inaccessible, spending most of the film at a remote sanitorium, cut off from Toru's college experience filled with demonstrations, classes, and parties. In contrast, Midori connects Toru to the present moment. She is very much part

Figure 4.1. Toru and Kizuki eat apples while
walking in Tokyo in *Norwegian Wood*.

Figure 4.2. Naoko appears like part of Toru's dream in *Norwegian Wood*.

of his college experience, and her outgoing nature and loquaciousness give her
physical presence in the film.

Notwithstanding the contrast between these two women, and the time
periods they represent, editing creates moments that merge past and present in
the film. Scenes inserted within the chronological ordering of the plot reveal the
way memory merges with material experience in cinematic representation as it
interrupts the here and now. A sequence that occurs when Toru visits Naoko at
the sanitorium reveals the confluence of the virtual and actual in time crystals. In
the scene, a shot of Toru falling asleep while waiting to meet Naoko in her quarters
is interrupted by a jump cut to Toru walking with Kizuki in Tokyo—most likely
a flashback, although the film does not clearly identify how the scene fits into the
timeline of the story. In this scene, a tracking shot captures Toru eating an apple
while he walks with Kizuki. The visceral sound of crunching provides a sense of

realism to the scene and an immediacy to the memory. As the scene jumps back to the sanitorium, Toru is awakened by Naoko, who appears before him, bathed in light as if she is part of a dream or memory. Although this moment with Naoko fits into the chronological ordering of the plot, the ethereal lighting used in the scene, in contrast to the tactile manner in which the memory of Kizuki is captured, renders the virtual and actual indistinguishable in Toru's mind. In that moment, the memory of Kizuki becomes part of the physical experience of the scene, while the encounter with Naoko becomes part of the memory.

Yet, if adaptations of Murakami's work deal with the confluence of the virtual and actual in the formation of personal memory, they also conflate personal memory with the larger historical imagination of both Japan and South Korea. Ichikawa's *Tony Takitani*, an adaptation of Murakami's 1990 story by the same name, presents a contemporary Japan in which the memory of World War II collapses into the experience of the present day, becoming inseparable from it. This merging of past and present is also the case with Lee's *Burning*, which translates the temporal experience of Murakami's fiction into a South Korean context through visual moments that figure a modern Korea very much informed by its fractured past. Both of these films rely on time crystals to translate the temporal experience of modernity in Murakami's fiction into a cinematic medium. In doing so, they present a reciprocal relationship between past and present, one that challenges the linear dimensions of rapid development that characterize the normative view of the history of both these traditions.

The tale of *Tony Takitani* demonstrates the way Japan's experience in World War II serves not as a step in the realization of the nation's developed status but as an enduring part of the contemporary cultural consciousness. Both the film and the story on which it is based tell of the title character, Tony Takitani, a baby boomer who grows up through the tumultuous decades after World War II, and his relationship with a strange woman who is obsessed with buying clothes. Tony's father, Shōzaburō, a jazz trombonist, lived and performed in Shanghai during the war but was locked up by the Chinese Army as the tide of the war shifted. Released from prison, Shōzaburō is sent back to Japan, where he marries a distant cousin, only to have his new wife die three days after giving birth to his first son. At a loss for what to name the boy, Shōzaburō decides to call him "Tony" after an American friend he met in the military. As he grows older, Tony cannot shake his ambivalence toward this American name given to him by his father:

> Tony was no name for a Japanese child, of course, but such a thought never crossed the major's mind. When Shōzaburō got home, he wrote the name Tony Takitani on a piece of paper and stuck it to the wall. He stared at it for the next several days. Tony Takitani. Not bad. Not bad. The American occupation of Japan was probably going to last awhile,

he thought, and an American-style name just might come in handy for the kid at some point. For the child himself, though, living with a name like that was not much fun. The other kids at school called him a "half-breed," and whenever he told people his name they responded with a look of puzzlement or distaste. Some people thought it was a bad joke, and others reacted with anger. For certain people, coming face to face with a child called Tony Takitani was all it took to reopen old wounds.[16]

Years later, after graduating from college, Tony marries a stylish woman with an obsession for trendy clothing. He grows to love her but becomes concerned with her tendency for impulsive shopping, a habit that tragically leads to her death in a car accident. After his wife passes away, Tony searches for a replacement for her. He hires a young assistant who looks like his wife, with the intention that she will wear some of the outfits his wife left behind. However, Tony is unable to go through with the agreement and instead spends hours in his wife's closet seeking to revive her memory by staring at her clothing:

These shadows had once clung to his wife's body, which had endowed them with the warm breath of life and made them move. Now, however, what hung before him were mere scruffy shadows, cut off from the roots of life and steadily withering away, devoid of any meaning whatsoever. Their rich colors danced in space like pollen rising from flowers, lodging in his eyes and ears and nostrils. The frills and buttons and lace and epaulets and pockets and belts sucked greedily at the room's air, thinning it out until he could hardly breathe. Liberal numbers of mothballs gave off a smell that might as well have been the sound of a million tiny, winged insects. He hated these dresses now, it suddenly occurred to him. Slumping against the wall, he folded his arms and closed his eyes. Loneliness seeped into him once again, like a lukewarm broth. It's all over now, he told himself. No matter what I do, it's over.[17]

Utilizing the resources of cinematic representation, Ichikawa's *Tony Takitani* depicts the divide between normative history and the experience of the past in the historical imagination. At first, history unfolds in linear dimensions, creating a clear divide between past and present in the film. The past is demarcated using color: the postwar period is visualized through black-and-white, sepia-toned photographs depicting Shōzaburō's life in the 1930s and 1940s, while Tony's experience in the present day is visualized through moving images in color. Likewise, the lateral flow of images across the screen throughout the film shows history unfolding sequentially, from past to present, according to the major periods of Tony's life. As the camera tracks to the right, vignettes from Tony's youth, college days, and adulthood unfold before the viewer.

In contrast to this linear ordering of events, time crystals depict this same period in nonlinear dimensions, manifesting through the overlapping that occurs between the material and the virtual—an effect, Deleuze argues, of the "actual optical image" crystallizing "with *its own* virtual image."[18] This doubling often appears in film through mirrors and reflections. "Time crystals [figure] as refracting, filtering, and reflecting surfaces in which the virtual and the actual are made visible and rendered indistinguishable as they pass into one another in the circuits of exchange."[19] Deleuze points to the films of German director Max Ophüls and American director Joseph Losey as examples of the way mirrors represent the exchange between the virtual "mirror image" and the actual form it reflects.[20] In Losey's *Eva* (1962), for instance, the liberal use of "oblique mirrors, concave and convex mirrors, and Vatinian mirrors" throughout the film reveal the way reflective surfaces meld material and fantasy.[21]

Along with manifesting through mirrors, time crystals are created through the doubling of characters. Alfred Hitchcock's *Vertigo* (1958), a film about memory and obsession, features a moment when the protagonist, Scottie, kisses his love interest, Judy, in her apartment. Suddenly, the floor begins to spin, and the location of the scene switches from Judy's apartment to the horse stables where Scottie earlier kissed Judy's look-alike, Madeleine, and then returns back to Judy's apartment. The movement between different backdrops without cutting problematizes attempts to give priority to the apartment as the real "material" present and to identify the stables as the virtual memory where Scottie recalls the earlier kiss. Instead, as the floor revolves, the kiss at the stable becomes part of the physical experience of Scottie's present, and the moment at the apartment becomes its virtual referent. By blending memory and matter, this moment allows multiple affects to condense and disperse in new ways in Scottie's, and the viewer's, mind, transcending the linear forms of recall often created between past and present.

Doubling occurs in both *Tony Takitani* and *Burning* to suggest the merging of the virtual and material in the experience of rapid development. In *Tony Takitani*, the two main actors play multiple roles: Ogata, as Tony and Shōzaburō, and Miyazawa, as Tony's wife (Eiko in the film) and his assistant (Hisako in the film). Having the same actor play both a character living in Japan's modern present and one from the past underscores the illusory nature of the teleology of development, leveling the division between an advanced contemporary Japan and its past. This merging of past and present is evident as Tony becomes obsessed with reviving Eiko's image after she dies, going so far as to require Hisako to wear her clothing in an attempt to meld the materiality of Hisako with his memory of Eiko. The blending of material and memory is also accomplished through dialogue. At first, there is a clear divide between the nondiegetic voice of the disembodied narrator—who describes Tony's life in the same manner that the third-person narrator relays

Tony's life in Murakami's story—and the diegetic voice of the characters. However, these two worlds collapse, as characters often repeat the narrator's lines or even speak in place of its disembodied voice, blending the objective world outside of the film with the fictional experiences within. Barbara Thornbury describes how this process breaks down the divide between audience and character, and between source text and cinematic adaptation:

> Linda Hutcheon (2006) has applied the term "knowing audience" to those who are already familiar with the material being adapted. Ichikawa embraces the knowing audience by often using exact phrases and sentences from Murakami's story in the third-person voice-over narration and in the characters' dialogue. A corollary to this is the way Ichikawa challenges conventional notions of narration and provocatively blurs the line between the diegetic and the non-diegetic aspects of the film: he has the actors playing Tony (child and adult), Eiko and Hisako on-screen and in character share in the narration by, for example, starting or completing the voice-over narrator's lines.[22]

Time crystals in *Tony Takitani*, moreover, are created through cinematography and editing. The linear unfolding of time enacted by the lateral movement of images across the screen is interrupted by moments that fuse present experience with the shadow of memory. Putting on Eiko's clothes is both a physical experience and a virtual one for Hisako, a brush with the "lingering shadow" of Eiko's memory. This lingering shadow, however, takes on material properties. The "weight" of the past physically overwhelms Hisako when she dresses in Eiko's clothes as part of her job interview. The memory of Tony's wife is so "heavy" that she cannot help but burst into tears.

As in Murakami's fiction, these moments take place in self-enclosed spaces, where characters experience the breakdown of the boundaries between self and other and past and present. Standing in for the dark wells, subterranean bars, and other liminal spaces in Murakami's fiction, Eiko's empty closet becomes a place where the virtual past is overlaid onto physical reality in a sequence after Tony sells all her clothing. The spatial aspects of Murakami's fiction are represented through match cuts and dissolves that merge memory and material experience. At the beginning of the scene, Tony is captured in the middle of the frame in a deep focus shot of the empty closet. A dissolve segues to Tony lying on the closet floor in the forefront of the frame, shot from the same position, suggesting the passing of time.

This early representation of linear time contrasts with the repetition created through matching, as the shot of Tony lying on the floor is matched with a shot of Shōzaburō lying in the same position in his prison cell during the war. The form cut on Tony's body, matched with that of his father, merges these two moments,

Figure 4.3. Tony sits in his wife's empty closet in *Tony Takitani*.

Figure 4.4. Tony lies in his wife's empty closet in *Tony Takitani*.

Figure 4.5. Tony lies in his wife's empty closet as
Hisako kneels beside him in *Tony Takitani.*

Figure 4.6. Tony's father, Shōzaburō, lies in his jail cell in *Tony Takitani.*

giving memory material presence in the film. The scene then cuts back to Tony's body, captured in the same deep focus shot that appeared at the start of the sequence. However, something has changed: the closet door, which was closed in the first shot, is now open, and white light streams in from outside. Although we assume this image indicates a return to the present in the timeline of the film, the lighting makes it appear as if the room is a dream, as if the space is not real but part of the world of imagination, cut off from the temporal sequence that initially gave structure to the scene. The scene then dissolves again to reveal Hisako crying in the middle of the frame while Tony lies in the forefront. Finally, the scene dissolves one more time to the original image of Tony lying on the floor of the closet with the door closed. By using form cuts and dissolves to layer virtual and actual images, the film disrupts the linear flow of the story, visualizing the transformation of the opaque materiality of the present—Eiko's closet of clothes—into a translucent prism that refracts memory.

In this way, time crystals in *Tony Takitani* challenge the othering of the past in linear models of development. Just as Hisako represents an amalgamation of the virtual memory of Tony's wife and the real woman living in the present, Tony represents a fusion of the person living in the present and the memory of the past, as depicted through his father. By portraying its leading characters in this way, the film represents a modern Japan that is not cut off from its past but rather formed through the virtual flows of memory that give shape to its material present.

Time crystals serve a central function in one of the most recent filmic adaptations of Murakami's work, *Burning* by Lee Chang-dong. As discussed above, the film is based on Murakami's 1983 short story "Barn Burning," which is itself based on the 1939 William Faulkner story of the same name. The Murakami tale involves a love triangle between the thirty-one-year-old protagonist, his bohemian girlfriend, and a wealthy young man, whom his girlfriend meets on a trip to Africa. The protagonist becomes obsessed with the young man, who claims to burn down barns in his free time. The story is left ambiguous as to whether the man is really an arsonist and/or whether he is a serial killer responsible for the disappearance of the protagonist's girlfriend.[23]

The localization of "Barn Burning" in South Korea is facilitated by the story's treatment of shared experiences with modernization.[24] Though more forced than the Japanese model, the rapid growth South Korea experienced after the Korean War (1950–1953), referred to as the "miracle on the Han River," mirrors Japan's dramatic progress during this same time. What is more, both traditions experienced the mixed feelings of pride and anxiety toward this development.[25] Pride in affluence and material advancement was accompanied by apprehensions about the way modernization required these traditions to fully embrace Western notions of progress, including the teleological trajectory through which development is thought to unfold.[26] The use of the term "miracle" to describe both of these nations' experiences with development speaks to the speed with which they were able to achieve the end goal of modernization: first-world status. At the same time, moving headlong into development required both these traditions to forget the strife and division that marked the early stages of growth; war, poverty, and political unrest were considered hurdles that these nations would successfully overcome to reach their end goals.

However, the superficial wealth that resulted from development, and the hollow designation of a "first-world country" that came with it, were not able to cover up the historical fractures that existed in the form of economic inequality, unemployment, debt, and civil unrest. For this reason, prosperity for both Japan and South Korea can often seem like an illusion, one that casts a shadow of doubt on the self-evidence of the contemporary experience. Kim suggests that Murakami's depiction of the ambivalence toward high-economic growth is a central reason for the popularity of his fiction in South Korea with the 386 generation, as discussed previously.[27]

As in *Tony Takitani*, the layer of affluence in the highly developed Seoul landscape in *Burning* is not enough to conceal the divisions that resulted in the realization of modernity. Hints of the fractures between the hypermodern present and the political activism of the 1980s are present throughout the film. The pieces of artwork on the walls of a fashionable museum in Seoul depict images of the student movements during the 1980s, a reminder of what was lost in the transition to first-world status. The division between the nation's agriculture-based economy prior to development and its current state of technological progress is evident in the inequality between the wealthy and the working class.[28] The reason Lee changed the protagonist from a thirtysomething urbanite in the Murakami story to a rural youth is because he wanted to capture the anger and repression that underprivileged members of the younger generation experience in South Korea and around the world. Images of a glitzy, hypermodern Seoul contrast sharply with the modest conditions of rural Paju, an agricultural city adjacent to the demilitarized zone located only an hour outside of the city that is undergoing dramatic transformations due to urbanization.[29] Finally, the sounds of North Korean propaganda audible in the rural setting of the film not far from Seoul call to mind conflicts of the past and national divisions that still loom in the cultural imagination. Fujiki Kosuke argues that the motif of invisibility in the film, demonstrated by the way North Korea is heard but never seen, reflects the divisions within the Korean peninsula:

> By employing such plot devices as an inexplicably disrupted phone call and the background sound of propaganda being broadcast through loudspeakers, Lee's film characterizes both the missing heroine and

North Korea itself as invisible: the former is a potential victim of serial killing, while the latter exists as an unseen enemy state believed to be a constant threat. By identifying and analyzing the film's motif of visibility and invisibility, this paper demonstrates how the tension between the protagonist and the antagonist parallels the longstanding geopolitical tension between the two Korean states.[30]

The characters in *Burning* reflect a division between Korea's rural past and the dizzying affluence of the present. Jongsu, a budding novelist from Paju, represents the working class of South Korea.[31] On his way to sell clothing in Seoul, Jongsu runs into a young woman he knew from high school, Haemi, who works as a sidewalk promoter for a department store in the city. The two begin to date, and Jongsu agrees to watch over Haemi's cat while she is away in Africa. When Jongsu meets her at the airport several weeks later, she is accompanied by a strange man, Ben, whom she met during her travels. Representing the superficiality of the nouveau riche lifestyle, Ben provides a stark contrast to Jongsu: he drives a Porsche, lives in an expensive condo, and leads a life of leisure. Fujiki argues that the animosity between Jongsu, who is part of the underclass, and Ben, who is rich, is the central source of tension in the film.[32] Ben figures as both the fantasy of new wealth in urban Seoul as well as a critique of the illusory nature of material excess in contemporary South Korea. Director Lee comments on how the hometowns of these two characters reflect current attitudes toward class in the country: "Jongsu in Paju, and Ben in Gangnam—the wealthiest, quietest, and most clean district of Korea—the two of them exist on opposite ends of the spectrum. But a lot of young people today live somewhere between these two poles. Many feel the helplessness that Jongsu feels, but they want to live like Ben. Some even assume that they are currently living like Ben."[33]

Like *Tony Takitani*, *Burning* complicates the linear temporality of modernization by underscoring the illusory experience of the affluent present as well as the material reality of the past. Time crystals form in the film through the blending of memory, fantasy, and physical phenomena, transforming virtual experiences into "real" ones. Haemi is the manifestation of both material and memory; she is the physical woman Jongsu meets in Seoul, the girl he remembers from his youth in rural Paju, and the woman of his fantasies. To anchor the viewer in the physical world at first, a cold open captures the hustle and bustle of a crowded shopping street in Seoul. A handheld camera follows Jongsu as he carries clothing into the department store where Haemi is working. The immediacy of the images depicted through naturalistic cinematography emphasizes the "realness" of the scene.

Yet, experience in this very real backdrop is also formed through the virtual dimensions of the past. Jongsu accesses Haemi through memory. She is connected to his home in rural Paju. When she goes missing partway through the film, he speculates she may have fallen into one of the many wells spread throughout the countryside, as she did when she was younger. Haemi is also a product of Jongsu's fantasy, a fantasy that begins when the two go to dinner on the night they meet in Seoul. When Jongsu returns to the table after paying the bill, he sees a couple kissing next to a sleeping Haemi, prompting him to see her as an object of his own sexual desire—a character in his fantasy. Even Haemi's cat, Boil, which Jongsu looks after while Haemi is away in Africa, manifests the transformation of a concept into a physical thing, a process that is foreshadowed when Haemi teaches Jongsu about pantomime, or the art of conjuring a physical experience out of something virtual. Although cats are forbidden in Haemi's apartment, and Boil is nowhere to be seen when Jongsu first visits her place, the cat nevertheless demands attention from Jongsu, who must clean up Boil's droppings on subsequent visits. It is not until the end of the film that Boil actually appears at Ben's apartment. In this way, Haemi is an amalgamation of Jongsu's physical experience in modern Seoul, his sexual fantasies, and his memory of his hometown.

Accordingly, Haemi transforms back and forth between an actual person and a virtual image. Her apartment near Seoul Tower serves as a place where memory and imagination become physical experience and where physical experience becomes part of fantasy through repetition. When Jongsu has sex with Haemi for the first time, the camera focuses on Jongsu, while Haemi's unresponsive body is left out of the frame. The camera then pans to capture Seoul Tower out of the window of the apartment, with a reverse shot showing Jongsu gazing at it. The details of this scene are important because this experience will be repeated later as fantasy, memory, and reality meld into one experience. While Haemi is in Africa, Jongsu goes to her apartment to feed her cat and stands in front of the same window, masturbating while recalling his sexual experience with her. Glancing at a photograph of Haemi on the wall, he turns his gaze to the tower, which serves as a physical reference point between his memory and fantasy. Later, we see an image of Jongsu and Haemi lying on Haemi's bed, with Haemi masturbating him from behind. However, just as Jongsu is about to climax, the camera cuts to reveal that he is alone on the bed.

Haemi's fluctuation between an actual image and a virtual abstraction visually manifests in a scene about halfway into the film, when she dances for Ben and Jongsu in front of Jongsu's Paju home. As the camera captures her dancing from behind, Haemi's dark silhouette floats against the horizon. Mimicking the shadow puppets she creates with her hands, Haemi loses distinctiveness as a character and becomes an abstraction, like the trees and brush that surround her. When she is finished dancing, Haemi too disappears, walking out of the frame as the camera remains in a static position. The scene ends with the camera panning to capture the landscape surrounding the home, without cutting back to show the viewer Haemi's location. Her disappearance from the frame reflects her vanishing from the story.

The relationship between Jongsu and Ben manifests a doubling effect that suggests the melding of past and present. As the affluent flip side to Jongsu's embodiment of South Korea's rural, working-class past, Ben becomes a virtual reflection of Jongsu. Because crystals are reflective surfaces, the doubling of the actual and virtual manifests through reflection, simulation, miming, and other forms of doubling.[34] Ben theorizes the existence of his own double, suggesting that he can exist simultaneously in different locations: "I am here, and I am there. . . . I am in Seoul, and I am in Africa." Accordingly, the one-dimensional Ben manifests as a foil for Jongsu throughout the film rather than as an independent character. He shows up as a third wheel just as Jongsu and Haemi's relationship begins to develop. His manner of interacting with others is odd; he never changes his expression or reacts in an emotional way, even when he is being killed by Jongsu at the end of the film. Ben is played by a Korean American actor, Steven Yeun, speaking in formal Korean, and both of these aspects accentuate Ben's unnatural presence in the film, as Lee mentions:

> I didn't really want to categorise the character of Ben as a second-generation Korean American, or someone who had spent his school time in the US, but despite all that, he does go by the name, Ben, and so, I think I was trying to go for, he has this westernised sort of feel, but it's also a familiar sort of presence in the film. For some reason—we're not really sure why—there are quite a bit of younger people in Korea now, who use a Western name, or use an English name, and have this Western sort of lifestyle that they're living . . . . For example, Steven's lines; he says them in perfect Korean, but there's that different something that you just can't put your finger on. There's something different, even though it is perfect Korean. In my opinion, I feel that that strengthens Steven's character, but of course, yes, these alien, sort of different qualities could definitely come out in his gestures, or expressions, but he is very much still in this film.[35]

Connections are drawn throughout the film between Ben and the title character of F. Scott Fitzgerald's *The Great Gatsby*, a text that is referenced in many Murakami stories. These connections reinforce Ben's role as an idea rather than a real person. With his superficial charm, Ben lives a life of leisure, yet the source of his fortune is never revealed. As Jongsu says, he is a Gatsby-like character because he is "a mysterious person who is young and rich," and yet "you don't know what [he] really [does]." As a Gatsby-like character, then, Ben reflects the fantasy of a rich urbanite and stands in stark contrast to Jongsu's experience as a poor farmer in the country.

Figure 4.7. Haemi dances in *Burning*.

Figure 4.8. Jongsu and Ben face off in *Burning*.

Ben's function as Jongsu's double is evident in scenes in which the two face off. Bergson suggests that experiencing the overlapping of the actual and virtual is like "actors watching themselves on stage."[36] Jongsu views his double when the two stand face-to-face in an elevator and when he crouches behind Ben on a hill overlooking the border to North Korea. Later, a shot-reverse shot captures Jongsu gazing up at Ben—who is in a luxury gym high above the city—from the street below. In this way, Jongsu's reflection through the image of Ben suggests the merging of past and present in the construction of identity in contemporary South Korea.

Ben's death at the end of the film demonstrates how the virtual and actual can exist in the same shot. In the final scene, Ben meets Jongsu on the side of a rural road. Arriving in his Porsche, Ben gets out of the car and approaches the truck in which Jongsu is sitting. As Jongsu gets out of the car, he suddenly stabs Ben, who recoils in pain. The fact that Jongsu is killing an abstraction is evident in Ben's inexpressiveness as he is being stabbed. Like Haemi, he does not react in a way that one would expect, refusing to scream or even speak during the encounter. At the same time, the visceral way in which the scene is shot suggests it is not just a fantasy but a real experience. As the two struggle, Ben falls to the ground and staggers toward his car. Just as Ben is climbing into his car, Jongsu catches up to him and sticks his knife into him one more time, killing him. Jongsu places Ben in the driver's seat and lights the car on fire, stripping down naked to toss his bloody clothes into the burning car. When Jongsu drives away, we see Ben's Porsche explode in the rearview mirror. This final inferno is the first fire depicted in the chronological ordering of the film but reminds the viewer of the greenhouses burning in Jongsu's imagination.

Ultimately, the doubling, replication, and overlapping of images in both *Tony Takitani* and *Burning* meld virtual and actual in cinematic adaptations of Murakami's fiction in South Korea and Japan. This focus on merging the virtual with the actual demonstrates a similar sense of anxiety toward the process of development in both these countries. Both Japan and Korea underwent modernization at different times and in different ways, but in their national histories, they both experienced the effects of moving through the early stages of modernity to arrive at economic prosperity in a short period of time. Certainly, the experience of developing so hastily can undermine the self-evidence of the developed status of both these traditions. It can make contemporary experience feel like an illusion while the suppressed aspects of the past—war, revolution, and political unrest—can return with a very real and present force, one that impacts the way Murakami is read and adapted in East Asia.

# 5

## Animating Haruki World:
## *Blind Willow, Sleeping Woman*

Even more than live-action cinema, animation provides the most fitting medium through which to capture the imaginative worlds of Murakami Haruki's fiction. Beginning with the documentary *Dreaming Murakami* (2017)—which focuses on the work of Murakami's Danish translator, Mette Holm—and including the recent feature by French animator Pierre Földes, *Blind Willow, Sleeping Woman* (2022), directors have utilized computer-generated images and different forms of animation to adapt Murakami's stories. Certainly, animation facilitates the visual representation of some of the more fantastic aspects of Murakami's work, like the giant talking frog that appears in "Super-Frog Saves Tokyo" ("Kaeru-kun, Tōkyō o sukū" [1999]). However, as the analysis of Földes's *Blind Willow, Sleeping Woman* demonstrates, it is the medium's capacity to blend ontologies that allows it to represent the in-betweenness of Murakami's writing and to capture the magical realism of his narratives while drawing meaning from the intertextuality of his stories. As this final chapter argues, the adaptation of Murakami's fiction into animation replicates Murakami's own literary project of blending worlds, characters, and stories to reveal something new.

Premiering in June 2022 at the Forty-Second Annecy International Film Festival in France, Földes's *Blind Willow, Sleeping Woman* embodies the blended ontologies of Murakami's work. Son of the renowned experimental animator Peter Földes, Pierre Földes comes from a blended artistic background himself, having worked as a composer and painter before trying his hand at animation with the shorts "Mikrodramas" (2009) and "Coffee and Bananas" (2012). *Blind Willow, Sleeping Woman* represents the realization of an eight-year project that Földes began on his own before eventually collaborating with France's Miyu

Studios. Like other directors who sought permission from Murakami to adapt his novels, Földes was granted the rights to some of Murakami's stories instead. He eventually decided to work with six stories. Two are anthologized in the 2002 collection *After the Quake* (*Kami no kodomo-tachi wa mina odoru* [2000)]: "Super-Frog Saves Tokyo" and "UFO in Kushiro" ("UFO ga Kushiro ni oriru"). Three are from the 2006 collection *Blind Willow, Sleeping Woman* (*Mekurayanagi to nemuru onna*). These are "Blind Willow, Sleeping Woman" ("Mekurayanagi to nemuru onna"), "Birthday Girl" ("Bāsudei gāru"), and "Dabchick" ("Kaitsuburi"). The last one is "The Wind-Up Bird and Tuesday's Women" ("Nejimaki-dori to kayōbi no onnatachi" [1986]), which serves as the basis of Murakami's novel *The Wind-Up Bird Chronicle* (1994–1995). Though many of the stories deal with the aftermath of the Great Hanshin Earthquake Disaster of 1995, which resulted in 6,433 casualties and over $100 billion in damages around the Kobe area, the stories were updated sixteen years later to speak to the aftermath of the even more destructive Tōhoku earthquake and tsunami on March 11, 2011 (3/11), which resulted in over twenty thousand casualties in northern seaside areas of Japan. Back in 1995, the shock of both the Great Hanshin Earthquake Disaster and the Tokyo subway gas attacks, which occurred within two months of each other, profoundly affected Japan, as Murakami suggests: "In some ways, the two events may be likened to the front and back of one massive explosion. Both were nightmarish eruptions beneath our feet—from underground—that threw all the latent contradictions and weak points of our society into frighteningly high relief."[1]

Földes sheds light on the postdisaster mentality of 3/11 by processing it through the lens provided by the stories Murakami wrote in reaction to the 1995 disaster. "UFO in Kushiro" tells of a man named Komura who agrees to transport a mysterious "black" box to Hokkaido for a friend after his wife, Kyōko, leaves him in the wake of the earthquake. There, he meets an unusual woman who manifests as Kyōko's doppelgänger. In "Super-Frog Saves Tokyo," a middle-aged Tokyo banker is recruited by an overgrown talking frog to save the city from a massive earthquake by doing battle with a giant subterranean worm that is responsible for other recent quakes. In addition to these pieces from *After the Quake*, Földes's film includes parts of several other stories by Murakami. "Blind Willow, Sleeping Woman" is told from the perspective of an unnamed adult narrator who accompanies his teenage cousin to the hospital for the cousin's ear treatment after a baseball injury left him with hearing loss. While waiting at the hospital for his cousin, the narrator is reminded of the time he accompanied his late best friend to the hospital to visit his friend's girlfriend, who was having minor surgery to correct an issue with one of her ribs. There, the girlfriend tells the story of a young woman sleeping in a house surrounded by so-called "blind willows," a tale that provides both the title of Földes's film as well as a motif for some of the more enigmatic dream sequences in it. "Birthday Girl" tells of a young waitress who, on her twentieth birthday, is granted one wish by the mysterious owner of the restaurant where she works. The protagonist of "Dabchick" gets lost in a Kafkaesque maze of hallways on his first day of work at a faceless corporation. Finally, in "The Wind-up Bird and Tuesday's Women," the narrator encounters a pushy telephone salesperson and a precocious thirteen-year-old neighbor while searching for his missing cat.

Brought together, these stories form a single narrative that takes place a few months after the 2011 Tōhoku disasters. Though Földes initially considered adapting the stories into a series of short films and compiling them into an anthology, he realized that merging them into one visual narrative would make more sense: "It was only later, while I was reworking my script, that I began to interpret characters from different short stories as multiple facets of the same characters, at different points in their lives. I like to think of my life so far as a series of short stories. And thus, little by little, the idea came to me to merge the stories and characters and combine them in a shared chronology."[2] After Murakami approved the plan, Földes created a screenplay that blended "UFO in Kushiro" and "Super-Frog Saves Tokyo" into one interconnected feature, combining the individual stories of the two main characters—Komura ("UFO") and Katagiri ("Super-Frog")—by having them work at the same bank in Tokyo.[3]

The adaptation *Blind Willow, Sleeping Woman* references Murakami's work by mixing aspects of mundane reality with fantastical experiences through an animation style that reflects the magical realism that has come to characterize the author's style. The film accomplishes this feat by blending the reality of live-action cinema with a more imaginary style of animation, making real character movement less real through rotoscoping while giving fantastical images grounding in reality. Földes speaks to the capacity of animation to relay the magical realist style he was hoping to capture in Murakami's work:

> This film is aimed not only at the millions of Murakami fans around the world, but also at a public into innovative storytelling which has been defined as magical realism, and for which animation is a great medium. Stories are made up of memories, dreams, and fantasies, influenced by individual visions of the earthquake—in the form of evil trees, a giant worm, a secret wish, an unknown password, a mysterious empty box, and dark endless corridors—in which the main characters try to reconnect with who they really are.[4]

Indeed, the story behind the creation of this animation style is as interesting as the final product itself, involving a hybrid process that included live-action shoots, 3D modeling, and classic 2D compositing.[5] The project began while Földes lived in Budapest, working on early treatments of animated stories about urban loneliness to use in his pitch to Murakami. In creating the initial treatment of his film, Földes forged his own style of animation by using the morph target functionality of Toon Boom software. A technique that Földes's own father developed decades earlier, morph target animation is a form of 3D computer simulation that allows animated images to morph into each other, creating the "ethereal" and "ultrafluid" effect that Földes thought would capture Murakami's style. In the early stages of the project, Földes periodically showed treatments of this animation style to Murakami, gaining the encouragement and approval of the author along the way. (Though the style of *Blind Willow, Sleeping Woman* would evolve over time, morphing techniques are still apparent throughout the film.)

After briefly stalling for a few months, the project resumed as a collaborative endeavor involving the work of thirty animators spread over four different locations in Europe and Canada: the film was produced by the French companies Cinéma Defacto and Miyu Productions and was coproduced by Studio MA, Arte France Cinéma, and Auvergne-Rhône-Alpes Cinéma; Canadian companies micro_scope and Production l'Unité Centrale; the Dutch company Original Picture; and the Luxemburg company Doghouse Films. As the project developed, Földes began experimenting with other techniques and shooting styles, including live action. In its final form, *Blind Willow, Sleeping Woman* is edited very much like a traditional film: most scenes began as live action before being animated except for a few parts of the dream sequences that required CGI (in particular, in one scene, the train on which Katagiri rides transforms into a giant worm, foreshadowing what is to come in the story, and in another, the frog leaves Katagiri's apartment by slipping through the cracks in his front door). After shooting live-action scenes, Földes rotoscoped over them to bring out the expressions of the characters, the "essential part of the film," he suggests.[6] However, the bodies of the actors that provide the basis for the characters were not only theirs, he points out, because he also used 3D sculpt software to form animated parts for characters like the frog, whose height made it difficult to represent through live capture. The animators used reference points provided by live action, exchanging the actors' heads for 3D models of the characters' faces, before tracing over the outline, reanimating their expressions, and coloring over the lines in the end. From there, the filmed footage and 3D models were composited to create the 2D production. A musician by training, Földes composed the soundtrack himself, using orchestral music with an electronic sound design that features piano.

The mixed style of *Blind Willow, Sleeping Woman* reflects the blended worlds that Murakami presents in his fiction while reinforcing the intertextual links that naturally arise in his oeuvre and expand the boundaries of his stories. At first, *Blind Willow, Sleeping Woman* emphasizes the oppressive nature of the mundane aspects of Murakami's stories and the way characters are trapped by the routines and institutions they experience every day. Muting the fantastic at first,

Figure 5.1. Katagiri is framed by elevator
doors in *Blind Willow, Sleeping Woman.*

Figure 5.2. A shot of Katagiri and Komura's
office in *Blind Willow, Sleeping Woman.*

cinematography, shot composition, editing, and other techniques of live-action
cinema make the setting of the film seem as ordinary as possible. After the film
opens in a subterranean tunnel, it transitions to Komura waking up from a bad
dream in his bedroom before it provides an inside-out establishing shot of Tokyo
and the title credits. The scene then jumps to an exterior shot of Komura's house
shrouded in darkness as the camera slowly pushes in before cutting to a shot inside
Komura's home again, capturing him walking into the living room, where his wife
stares at images of the 3/11 disaster broadcast on TV. We then cut to a motif that
Földes uses throughout the film to capture the experience of confinement: a frame-
within-frame shot of Komura looking out the window of his home.

As the action shifts to Komura and Katagiri's workspace, the cinematography used to depict office life reinforces the stark reality of their mundane conditions. A scene that takes place at Tokyo Security Trust Bank, where they both work, opens with a low-angle shot of the building looming over the camera, demonstrating its real and oppressive presence in the lives of the characters. The scene cuts to a high angle shot of Katagiri being reprimanded by his boss as he cowers helplessly against the wall of his cubicle, his boss blocking his escape. A shot-reverse shot underscores this feeling of dread as it cuts back and forth between his boss's angry face and Katagiri's bowing head. Shot compositions of the background of the cubicles in the office are mostly composed of geometric lines that reflect the regimented nature of corporate life, while the washed-out colors used to animate the mise-en-scène manifests its homogeneity. Later, elevator doors form a frame within frame that traps Katagiri as he rides up the lift with other coworkers.

Breaking up these scenes of everyday office life are dream sequences that Komura and Katagiri experience while on trains, showcasing a fantasy world that is other to their daily lives. In the first sequence, Katagiri is captured front on as he sleeps on a crowded commuter train on his way to work. As the train moves across the screen from right to left, images of Tokyo are shown in the background. The camera pushes in to an extreme close-up of his face before dissolving to show Katagiri's dream—an image of him floating vertically across the screen inside of a giant transparent worm that flies along in the same direction as the train. In contrast to the more realistic depiction of the train's movements, the worm glides effortlessly above the tracks. Later, as Komura snoozes on a train taking him back to his hometown, his dream of venturing into a nightmarish forest is relayed by a POV shot that visualizes a surreal landscape in which his missing cat appears in blue. As he follows the cat into a grove of trees, he sees a woman sitting on a chair, petting the cat in her arms—a scene that will be repeated later in the film. As the woman looks up, he retreats, and the scene transitions to a bird's-eye shot of the train traveling through a forest.[7] These fantasy sequences conjured through more imaginative forms of animation, then, point to worlds existing beyond an everyday reality depicted through more conventional forms of animation.

However, just like in a Murakami novel, real and imaginary begin to blur. The fantasy sequences that both characters encounter first in their dreams, apart from their waking life, begin to invade the reality of their existence. In the very next scene, Katagiri returns to his apartment to find a gigantic frog standing inside. As the frog speaks, its British accent, impeccable manners, and erudite knowledge of the literary classics belies the cartoonish image through which it manifests. (The frog cites a number of quotes, like Nietzsche's "the greatest wisdom is to be afraid of nothing" and Hemingway's "the real value of our existence is determined not by our victories, but by our defeats.") Though the animated medium makes this intrusion of the fantastic more palatable and less abrupt than it might be in live action, it nevertheless creates a contrast from the realistic style of animation used to capture these types of scenes. This scene is not a normal happening in the world of the film, and yet it is told in such a matter-of-fact way that viewers are meant to accept it at face value, as the frog informs Katagiri: "I know that you are thinking that I must be mad or you are having some kind of dream, but I am not crazy, and you are not dreaming. This is positively serious." Furthermore, a sequence explaining the threat that the worm poses to Tokyo plays in an abstracted style of animation, creating a contrast from the mise-en-scène of the main diegetic world and solidifying the worm's place in the consensual reality presented in the film.

The use of an animated frog to relay the magical realism of Murakami's fiction is also apparent in another film about translating Murakami's works, *Dreaming Murakami*. Directed by Nitesh Anjaan, the documentary depicts the work of Mette Holm, Murakami's Danish translator, to relay the meaning and spirit of Murakami's *Hear the Wind Sing* in Danish. The effort to translate the novel takes Holm to Japan, where she reads Murakami at Denny's, like characters in *After Dark*; talks with readers in small bars, like the ones that appear in *Hear the Wind Sing*; learns about pinball machines so she can accurately translate scenes involving the bar game; and meets with German and Polish translators of the Japanese author to learn of their techniques in capturing his tone. In particular, she fixates on the enigmatic first line of *Hear the Wind Sing*: "There is no such thing as perfect writing, just as there is no such thing as perfect despair." Wrestling with the many different ways to interpret this statement, Holm acknowledges the porous boundaries between the two languages, Japanese and Danish, and between her identity and function as a translator, and Murakami's as a writer. To capture this sense of in-betweenness, Anjaan places a computer-generated frog in various scenes in the film, creating a jarring effect that stands out more in live action than in the animated style of *Blind Willow, Sleeping Woman*. The image of this animated frog following Holm through train stations, playgrounds, and city streets perfectly captures the "Murakami moments" that Holm identifies in the author's work, in which something fantastic happens in the middle of everyday life, and the boundaries separating worlds, realities, and languages dissolve.

The rendering of characters using live action, rotoscoping, and 2D animation, moreover, continually disrupts divisions between reality and imagination. Including live action in the production allowed Földes to capture the mannerisms and expressions of actors as a way of bringing out the layers of human sentiment in Murakami's work, something that would be difficult to achieve through pure animation.[8] In fact, Földes suggests he intended for the film to be more "composited" in its final form, as he sought, before changing his mind, to self-consciously reproduce characters and scenery as pixilated images within the film

Figure 5.3. The dark forest into which Komura
ventures in *Blind Willow, Sleeping Woman*.

Figure 5.4. Frog visits Katagiri's apartment
in *Blind Willow, Sleeping Woman*.

to foreground its status as an assemblage of mediums. Földes's choice to use live
action to provide a reference point in the final production, in contrast, allows the
effects of both these mediums to impact the visual presentation of the film. The
rotoscoped character who descends a spiral staircase in the subterranean scene
that opens the film lends kinesthetic reality to the animated veneer of the image, as
he carefully steps down each stair and brushes his hand against the wall.

Furthermore, the live-action mannerisms and gestures of actors create reference points that provide the weight of real human interaction, bringing out the emotional subtext of the story in a way that might be lost through the weightlessness of purely animated images. In the second section of the film, based on the story "Blind Willow, Sleeping Woman," blocking and body movement provide insights into deeper sentiments lurking beneath the casual chitchat of Komura and his cousin as they travel to the hospital. Capturing the two standing at a bus stop, a front-on wide shot reveals the emotional distance separating the topic of their conversation from the boy's true feelings—his apprehension concerning treatment for hearing loss. As they get on the bus, the two are again placed in a position that creates a sense of distance with their backs to the viewer as they look out the window. When the camera jumps to the other side to face the characters, the conversation grows serious, broaching the boy's anxiety. As he discusses his fear, the boy's discomfort is apparent through subtle body movements, while Komura's exaggerated mannerisms demonstrate his efforts to reassure his cousin. Later, as Komura sits with his cousin in the hospital's waiting room, the camera pulls in close to capture the pain that Komura feels as he relays his experience visiting Kyōko at the hospital, before the two were married.

Likewise, shot composition and editing accentuate the realistic impression given by the rotoscoped images. The film relies on two common cinematic techniques—frame within framing and shot-reverse shots—to draw our attention to the understated gestures that develop characters and their relationships with others. When Komura travels to Hokkaido to deliver the mysterious box, he meets two women—the sister of the coworker who asked him to deliver the box, Keiko, and her friend, Shimao—who appear like twins waiting for him in the arrival area of the airport. His interaction with the women accentuates his feelings of displacement from his home in Tokyo, mirroring the dislocation the rest of the country experienced after the disaster. Right from the time they meet, reverse shots from the back of the two women standing next to each other frame Komura's face, drawing attention to the sorrow he feels about being abandoned by his wife. Mistakenly believing that Komura's wife died, they express their condolences, to which Komura reacts with both palatable shame and embarrassment. The depiction of Shimao's mannerisms, in particular, plays a central role in story development. Her animated interaction with Komura creates a stark contrast to his relationship with Kyōko, allowing him to find the intimate connection he lacked in his marriage. As the two discuss Komura's wife and the malaise resulting from long-distance travel, Shimao shrugs her shoulders, brushes her hair behind her ears, and nods her head as she listens emphatically to Komura's story. Later, as the two sit on Komura's hotel bed talking, Shimao's mannerisms grow even more expressive as she uses her whole body to flirt with Komura—playing with her hair, laughing, and raising her arms in exaggerated movements.

While the blending of mediums and styles in *Blind Willow, Sleeping Woman* reflects Murakami's own efforts to merge realities in his fiction, it also develops Murakami's literary worlds by revealing the intertextual links that connect disparate works. Combining several stories into one narrative required Földes to serve as a collaborator and even coauthor in the creation of a new story, as he worked to identify nodal points across the six selected stories on which he could build a longer narrative. To create a center for the film, Földes focused on the treatment of disaster in *After the Quake*, and references to the earthquake emerge throughout the movie. Footage of the quake and tsunami, and scientific reports detailing the workings of plate tectonics and hydrodynamics at its basis, play on televisions in Komura's home, in his office, in the cafeteria where he dines with his coworkers, and even in the hotel where he stays with Shimao in Hokkaido. What is more, the film uses the earthquake to provide thematic material, focusing not only on the rupturing of the ground in Japan but also the rupturing of relationships in its aftermath.

And yet Földes also develops new understandings of Murakami's work by unearthing intertextual motifs that manifest across his oeuvre, inviting connections that develop beyond the limits of individual stories and novels. Földes's work to traverse Murakami's texts replicates the narrative function personified in the translators and authors that emerge as characters in his fiction. Like K in *Sputnik Sweetheart* (1999) and Tengo in *1Q84* (2011), Földes serves as a ghostwriter, assimilating motifs that reoccur in Murakami's works—wives that leave home, love triangles, and the magical realism of suburban life—and weaving them together into one cohesive tale. One central motif Földes draws upon is the use of hotel rooms and dense forests to serve as portals to different realities. Hotels emerge throughout Murakami's oeuvre, most famously in the image of the Dolphin Hotel from *A Wild Sheep Chase* and its sequel, *Dance Dance Dance* (1988), in which the boutique inn transforms into a massive resort that serves as a site for supernatural happenings. Hotels also emerge in *The Wind-Up Bird Chronicle* as a representation of the metaphysical realm to which the protagonist ventures to find his wife. The motif of wandering through forests comes from *A Wild Sheep Chase*, as the narrator searches for a mysterious cabin in the Hokkaido countryside to locate a sheep with a star on its back, and *Kafka on the Shore* (2005), in which the protagonist ventures into the woods to discover the truth of his family history. True to their function in Murakami's writing, hotels and forests in *Blind Willow, Sleeping Woman* provide places to which characters travel to locate something missing. For example, Hotel Astral creates the setting for Kyōko's birthday wish, the hotel in Hokkaido is the place where Komura gets in touch with other aspects of his estranged wife, and the mysterious forest that Komura sees in his dream leads him to visages of his wife and cat, both of whom he finds hidden in its depths. Preparing characters to enter these different realms, the paths through which they pass reorient their temporal and ontological experiences. The darkness of the underground passage at the start of the film contrasts to the world above the street. Additionally, the artificial lighting of the hallway that leads Kyōko to the fateful hotel room, as well as the narrow alleyway overgrown with brush into which Komura ventures to find his lost cat, appear as places cut off from the flow of time. Even the plane ride that Komura takes to deliver the package in Hokkaido distorts his geographical and temporal senses.

Reinforcing his position as coauthor of a Murakami story, Földes blends characters from different stories into one narrative world, a process that reflects Murakami's own assimilation of characters through the many doppelgängers that appear in his stories. The idea of a doppelgänger, discussed at length previously, facilitates the linking of different stories in Murakami's oeuvre and the characters who inhabit them because of the way that doubles often manifest as ambiguous characters whose attributes could be shared by many different individuals. Doubles capture the spirit of Murakami's works because the author often uses generic character types across several different novels: the protagonist of his first four novels is the same narrative persona, while subsequent novels incorporate a similar voice even if they do not make specific connections to protagonists of earlier works. Animation aids in the representation of doubles because of its capacity to capture a range of people in one image without fleshing out a specific person. Kyōko and her doppelgängers are abstracted images that lack the particular attributes that define a person, thus allowing characters not to be totally different from, and not to be totally the same as, others.

The use of doppelgängers in animation reveals the way characters blend together across Murakami's worlds. Földes acknowledges this motif in Murakami's work by drawing our attention to the doubles that exist in "UFO in Kushiro." In the film *Blind Willow, Sleeping Woman*, other women that Komura runs across appear as doubles for Kyōko; they provide a new dimension of his wife that Komura does not normally encounter, manifesting opposing traits that Komura associates with Kyōko. While Kyōko is withdrawn, laconic, and frigid, Shimao is outgoing, talkative, and sexually aggressive. And yet, the two repeat the same lines: speaking with Komura in Hokkaido, Shimao echoes Kyōko's comments about the capacity for people to change—"no matter what you wish for, no matter how far you go, you can never be anything but yourself." Likewise, while the jaded Kyōko seems overwhelmed by the tragic events of her own life and the larger cultural landscape, the precocious yet naive young girl Komura meets as he searches for his cat represents a more innocent version of his wife.

However, Földes also expands Murakami's experimentation with doppelgängers through the development of characters across his literary works. Merging several stories into one inevitably leaves fault lines in the larger narrative, much like those that ruptured the ground after the earthquake depicted in the film. These fractures necessitate the rewriting of story elements and the development of characters to allow source texts to blend seamlessly. Reducing six main characters into just three protagonists—Komura, Kyōko, and Katagiri—requires unifying the characters: Komura serves as an amalgamation of the protagonists of "Blind Willow, Sleeping Woman," "Dabchick," and "The Wind-Up Bird and Tuesday's Women," while Kyōko combines the main characters in "Birthday Girl" and "The Wind-Up Bird and Tuesday's Women" to create Komura's counterpart in the story. The film positions Komura as the protagonist of "Blind Willow, Sleeping Woman" and reframes the events of the story so they occur after Kyōko leaves him and he heads to his hometown to spend time with family. While there, he takes his cousin to the hospital and reminisces about visiting his best friend's girlfriend in the hospital, who, though nameless in the original story, fuses with Kyōko in the film, providing the backstory for their relationship. Finally, Kyōko becomes one with the main character in "Birthday Girl," and Komura merges with the protagonist of "The Wind-up Bird and Tuesday's Women," whose wife also leaves him.

Along with collapsing these characters, the film blends the worlds of "UFO in Kushiro" and "Super-Frog Saves Tokyo" into one universe involving protagonists who work at the same company, even though Komura has a different occupation—a hi-fi equipment salesman—in "UFO in Kushiro." Putting Katagiri and Komura in the same universe requires tweaking the plot so that their stories intertwine. In the film, the two brush up against each other early when Komura delivers files to Katagiri after he is scolded by his boss. They do so again at the end of the film, as the boss interrupts his meeting with Katagiri to answer a phone call from Komura. From "Dabchick," Földes borrows the rigid, top-down bureaucracy of contemporary corporate life that traps both Komura and Katagiri, as evidenced by the use of tight, frame-within-frame shots to depict the two at work. Furthermore, the film changes the resolution of the men's stories in order to figure them as contrasting characters. As a reward for successfully resisting the attempts of gangsters to defraud his company, Katagiri is given a raise by his boss in the midst of layoffs and buyouts that are occurring at the company, providing a resolution more befitting a feature film than the one offered by the short story. In contrast, Komura chooses to take the buyout offered by his boss at the end of the film, creating a rationale for the unemployed status of the protagonist of "The Wind-Up Bird and Tuesday's Women," for whom he doubles at the end. To create cohesion in the narrative, furthermore, the disparate parts of the story are interlocked through the use of parallel advances, flashbacks, and dream sequences that anticipate narrative developments while crystalizing main themes.

Yet, it is the rewriting of Kyōko's story that requires the most invention on the part of Földes. Not fleshed out as a character in "UFO in Kushiro," Kyōko

Figure 5.5. Shimao flirts with Komura
in *Blind Willow, Sleeping Woman*.

Figure 5.6. Komura ventures down the alleyway behind
his home in *Blind Willow, Sleeping Woman*.

is given more of a backstory to fill out the longer narrative arc of the film by
merging her with the protagonist of "Birthday Girl" and making her the girlfriend
of Hiroshi, the narrator's best friend in "Blind Willow, Sleeping Woman." "Blind
Willow, Sleeping Woman," "Birthday Girl," and "The Wind-Up Bird and Tuesday's
Women," moreover, are used to bring new insights into the relationship between
Komura and Kyōko. The film explains that Kyōko moved to Tokyo after Hiroshi
died, referencing the plot of "Blind Willow, Sleeping Woman," and Komura, who
is secretly in love with Kyōko, followed her. She knew he was in love with her,
and she let him take care of her even though she did not love him in the same

Figure 5.7. Komura and his teenage neighbor chat
in *Blind Willow, Sleeping Woman*.

way she loved Hiroshi. While in Tokyo, she works at the Italian restaurant, where the magical experience happens on her birthday. After quitting her job, though, she moves in with Komura, and the two get married, as is explained in the film. Inventing a backstory for Kyōko that explains why she left Komura develops Murakami's writing in new directions. Murakami was accused, at least early in his career, of creating one-dimensional female characters who mysteriously disappear from the story when they are no longer needed. Developing story elements that are both in harmony with Murakami's work and also new to it solidifies Földes's role as a cocreator, not just adaptor, of Murakami's writing.

In this way, merging characters, motifs, storylines, and even historical periods from six different stories into one animated film opens up Murakami's texts, developing their meaning beyond their original form. More than the replication of Murakami's idiosyncratic voice and characters with which readers around the world are familiar, it is this very act of blending that most closely references Murakami's literary project. After all, Murakami's stories reveal the transformation of his characters into multiple doppelgängers, the development of overlapping worlds through a magical realist style, the merging of material experience and memory, and the mixing of genre styles like science fiction and detective literature. For Murakami, stories do not originate on one side of the exchange between readers and artists, as the analysis of cinematic adaptations in this book demonstrates. Rather, stories are the product of the very movement back and forth between those who read, translate, and adapt Murakami's work, originating and existing, ultimately, in the space between these transactions.

# Filmography

### *Blind Willow, Sleeping Woman (Saules aveugles, femme endormie* [2022])

France
Director: Pierre Földes
Production Company: Miyu Productions, Cinéma Defacto, Doghouse Films, micro_scope, Productions l'Unite Centrale, Original Picture, Arte France Cinéma, Auvergne-Rhône-Alpes Cinéma, Studio MA
Producer: Pierre Baussaron, Tom Dercourt, Emmanuel-Alain Raynal, Pierre Urbain, David Mouraire
Screenplay: Pierre Földes
Cinematographer: Étienne Boilard
Editor: Kara Blake
Cast: Katharine King So, Shoshana Wilder, Jesse Noah Gruman
Color. 100 min.

### *Drive My Car (Doraibu mai kā* [2021])

Japan
Director: Hamaguchi Ryūsuke
Production Company: Bitters End
Producer: Yamamoto Teruhisa
Screenplay: Hamaguchi Ryūsuke, Ōe Takamasa
Cinematographer: Shinomiya Hidetoshi
Editor: Yamazaki Azusa
Cast: Nishijima Hidetoshi, Miura Tōko, Okada Masaki
Color. 179 min.

### Burning (Beoning [2018])

South Korea, Japan
Director: Lee Chang-dong
Production Company: Pine House Film, NHK, Now Films
Producer: Lee Chang-dong, Lee Joon-dong, Ok Gwang-hee
Screenplay: Oh Jungmi, Lee Chang-dong
Cinematographer: Hong Kyung-pyo
Editor: Kim Da-won, Kim Hyun
Cast: Yoo Ah-in, Steven Yeun, Jong-seo Jeon
Color. 148 min.

### Hanalei Bay (Hanarei bei [2018])

Japan
Director: Matsunaga Daishi
Production Company: TalkStory Productions
Producer: Hashimoto Ryūta, Jason K. Lau, Ozawa Shinji
Screenplay: Matsunaga Daishi
Cinematographer: Kondō Ryūto
Editor: Matsunaga Daishi
Cast: Yoshida Yō, Sano Reo, Murakami Nijirō
Color. 97 min.

### Dreaming Murakami (2017)

Denmark
Director: Nitesh Anjaan
Production Company: Final Cut for Real
Producer: Signe Byrge Sørensen, Pernille Tornøe
Cinematographer: Agapi Triantafillidis
Editors: Denniz Göl Bertelsen, Nikoline Løgstrup
Cast: Mette Holm
Color. 58 min.

### The 100% Perfect Girl (2015)

United States
Director: Johan Stavsjö
Producer: Grant Crawford, Johan Stavsjö
Screenplay: Johan Stavsjö
Cinematographer: Marcus Fahey.  Editor: Johan Stavsjö
Cast: Quinn Corcoran, Grant Crawford, Shea LaManque, Ivana Méndez,
  Johan Stavsjö
Color. 14 min.

### Gorzko! (Bittersweet [2014])

Poland
Director: Michal Wawrzecki
Production Company: Krzysztof Kieslowski Faculty of Radio and Television
University of Silesia in Katowice
Screenplay: Michal Wawrzecki
Cinematographer: Cezary Stolecki
Editor: Michal Zytkowski
Cast: Anna Gorajska, Piotr Polak, Hanna Maciag
Color, Black and White. 19 min.
https://vimeo.com/86035510

### The Diary of Sounds (Shchodennyk zvukiv [2012])

Ukraine
Director: Glib Luukianets
Production Company: Moskit, Propeller Studios, a.steroid
Producer: Maria Donchik, Glib Luukianets
Screenplay: Glib Luukianets, Anton Kasian, Marta Molfar
Cinematographer: Timur Minazirov
Cast: Alexander Zinevich, Nikita Petrov, Taras Borovyk
Color. 28 min.

### Acoustic (Eokuseutig [2010])

South Korea
Director: You Sang-Hun
Producer: Kim Myeongeun, Song Chanho
Cinematographer: Song Ho-yeon
Editor: Son Byeong-chae, Lee Dong-hun
Cast: Shin Se-gyung, Im Jun-il, Lee Dong-hyun
Color. 88 min.

### The Second Bakery Attack (2010)

Mexico, United States
Director: Carlos Cuarón
Production Company: BN Films, Bonita Films, surDream Productions
Producer: Alfonso Cuarón, Dan Carrillo Levy
Screenplay: Carlos Cuarón
Cinematographer: Terry Stacey
Editor: Carlos Armella
Cast: Kirsten Dunst, Brian Geraghty, Lucas Akoskin
Color. 10 min.

### Norwegian Wood (Noruwei no mori [2010])

Japan
Director: Trần Anh Hùng
Production Company: Asmik Ace Entertainment, Dentsu, Fuji Television
Network, Kōdansha, Sankei Shimbun, Sumitomo Corporation, WOWOW
Producer: Kameyama Chihiro, Wouter Barendrecht, Teshima Masao,
  Michael J. Werner
Screenplay: Trần Anh Hùng
Cinematographer: Lee Ping Bin
Editor: Mario Battistel
Cast: Matsuyama Ken'ichi, Kikuchi Rinko, Mizuhara Kiko
Color. 133 min.

### All God's Children Can Dance (2008)

United States
Director: Robert Logevall
Production Company: Anonymous Content, Sidney Kimmel Entertainment
Producer: Bruce Toll
Screenplay: Scott Coffey
Cinematographer: Giorgio Scali
Editor: Mitchell Sinoway
Cast: Joan Chen, Jason Lew, Sonja Kinski
Color. 85 min.

### Tony Takitani (Tonī Takitani [2004])

Japan
Director: Ichikawa Jun
Production Company: Breath, Wilco Co.
Producer: Yonezawa Keiko
Screenplay: Ichikawa Jun
Cinematographer: Hirokawa Taishi
Editor: Sanjo Tomoh
Cast: Ogata Issey, Miyazawa Rie, Takahumi Shinohara, Nishijima Hidetoshi
Color. 75 min.

### Dancing with Dwarves (Dansa med dvärgar [2003])

Sweden
Director: Emelie Carlsson Gras
Production Company: Filmpool Nord
Producer: Emelie Carlsson Gras
Screenplay: Emelie Carlsson Gras

Short Story: Murakami Haruki
Cinematographer: Mattias Staley
Editor: Emelie Carlsson Gras, Torgny Schunnesson
Cast: Sara Lindh, Keijo Salmela, Ivan Mathias Petersson, Mikael Stålnacke
Black and White. 14 mins.

## The Other Side of the Forest (Mori no mukōgawa [1988])

Japan
Director: Nomura Keiichi
Producer: Shimizu Kazuo
Screenplay: Nakamura Tsutomu
Novel: Murakami Haruki
Cinematographer: Andō Shōhei
Editor: Taniguchi Toshio
Cast: Fujita Susumu, Isshiki Saiko, Kitayama Osamu, Miyake Kuniko,
  Terada Minori
Color. 75 min.

## A Girl, She Is 100% (100% no onna no ko [1983])

Japan
Director: Yamakawa Naoto
Producer: Kato Masayasu
Screenplay: Yamakawa Naoto
Cinematographer: Yamakawa Naoto
Editor: Yamakawa Naoto
Cast: Yoshinari Kumamoto, Muroi Shigeru, Sakaguchi Kazunao,
  Yamaguchi Akifumi
Color, Black and White. 12 min.

## Attack on a Bakery (Pan'ya shūgeki [1982])

Japan
Director: Yamakawa Naoto
Production Company: Beach Flash
Producer: Masamichi Shimojo
Screenplay: Yamakawa Naoto
Cast: Bang-ho Cho, Suwa Taro, Muroi Shigeru
Black and White. 17 min.

### Hear the Song of the Wind (*Kaze no uta o kike* [1982])

Japan
Director: Ōmori Kazuki
Production Company: Art Theatre Guild, Cinema House
Producer: Taga Shosuke
Screenplay: Ōmori Kazuki
Cinematographer: Watanabe Kenji
Editor: Yoshida Eiko
Cast: Kobayashi Kaoru, Shingyōji Kimie
Color.. 98 min.

# Bibliography

Aguilar, Carlos. "He Made One of the Year's Most Acclaimed Movies. Ryûsuke Hamaguchi Talks about 'Drive My Car.'" *Los Angeles Times*, December 20, 2021. https://www.latimes.com/entertainment-arts/movies/story/2021-12-20/drive-my-car-explained-ryusuke-hamaguchi-interview.

Baik, Jiwoon. "Murakami Haruki and the Historical Memory of East Asia." *Inter-Asia Cultural Studies* 11, no. 1 (2010): 64–72.

Bergson, Henri. *Matter and Memory*. Translated by Nancy Margret Paul and W. Scott Palmer. New York: Macmillan, 1913.

Berlatsky, Eric. *The Real, the True, and the Told: Postmodern Historical Narrative and the Ethics of Representation*. Columbus: Ohio State University Press, 2011.

Bogue, Ronald. *Deleuze on Cinema*. New York: Routledge, 2003.

Cassegård, Carl. "Murakami Haruki and the Naturalization of Modernity." *International Journal of Japanese Sociology* 10, no. 1 (December 2002): 80–92.

Cattrysse, Patrick, "Film (Adaptation) as Translation: Some Methodological Proposals," *Target* 4, no. 1 (2022): 53–70.

Clerici, Nathan, "History, 'Subcultural Imagination,' and the Enduring Appeal of Murakami Haruki." *The Journal of Japanese Studies* 42, no. 2 (Summer 2016): 247–278.

Colebrook, Claire. *Gilles Deleuze*. New York: Routledge, 2002.

Croll, Ben. "Miyu Adapts Haruki Murakami Stories with Novel Animation Technique in 'Blind Willow, Sleeping Woman.'" *Variety*, June 19, 2021. https://variety.com/2021/film/global/annecy-miyu-productions-murakami-blind-willow-sleeping-woman-1235000603/.

Deleuze, Gilles. *Cinema 2: The Time-Image*. Translated by Hugh Tomlinson and Robert Galeta. New York: Continuum Books, 1985.

Fisher, Russ. "First Look: Kirsten Dunst in Carlos Cuarón's 'The Second Bakery Attack.'" *Slashfilm*, November 29, 2010. https://www.slashfilm.com/512433/kirsten-dunst-carlos-cuarns-the-bakery-attack/?utm_campaign=clip.

Fujiki, Kosuke. "Adapting Ambiguity, Placing (In)visibility: Geopolitical and Sexual Tension in Lee Chang-dong's *Burning*." *Cinema Studies* 14 (2019). https://www.jstage.jst.go.jp/article/jscsj/14/0/14_72/_article.

Gerow, Aaron. "Murakami Haruki ni okeru eiga to bungaku no kōryū" [The relationship between film and literature in the work of Murakami Haruki]. In *Murakami Haruki: A Journey into Movies*, edited by the Tsubouchi Memorial Theatre Museum, Waseda University, 86–90. Tokyo: the Tsubouchi Memorial Theatre Museum, Waseda University, 2022.

Greene, Barbara. "Alienation and *After Dark*." *Critique: Studies in Contemporary Fiction* 62, no. 1 (2020): 1–15.

Hamaguchi, Ryūsuke and Łukasz Mańkowski. "On the Road with Hamaguchi Ryūsuke." *Sight and Sound*, November 16, 2021. https://www.bfi.org.uk/sight-and-sound/interviews/hamaguchi-ryusuke-drive-my-car.

Hansen, Gitte Marianne and Michael Tsang. "Politics in/of Transmediality in Murakami Haruki's Bakery Attack Stories." *Japan Forum* 32, no. 3 (2020): 404–431.

Hayashi, Keisuke. "Murakami Haruki bungaku ni okeru sai hon'yaku o tsūjita sōsaku no hōhō" [A proposal of a new Japanese language pedagogy through the use of back-translation in the literature of Haruki Murakami]. *The Nineteenth Princeton Japanese Pedagogy Forum: Proceedings; May 2012*. Princeton: Department of East Asian Studies, Princeton University, 2012, 30–39.

Hsu, Irene. "How *Burning* Captures the Toll of Extreme Inequality in Korea." *Atlantic*, November 15, 2018. https://www.theatlantic.com/entertainment/archive/2018/11/burning-movie-imagines-working-class-anxiety-south-korea-lee-chang-dong/575773/.

Hutcheon, Linda. *A Theory of Adaptation*. Oxford: Routledge, 2012.

Inata, Shino. *DVD BOOKLET Panya shūgeki*. Directed by Yamakawa Naoto. Tokyo: Cinema Brain, 2001.

Ishii-Kuntz, Masako. "Balancing Fatherhood and Work: Emergence of Diverse Masculinities in Japan." In *Men and Masculinities in Contemporary Japan. Dislocating the Salaryman Doxa*, edited by James E. Robinson and Nobue Suzuki, 198–216. New York: Routledge Curzon, 2003.

Kasman, Daniel. "Mysterious Elements: Lee Chang-dong Discusses *Burning*." *Mubi: Notebook Interview*, May 29, 2018. https://mubi.com/notebook/posts/mysterious-elements-lee-chang-dong-discusses-burning.

Katō, Norihiro, "Bungaku chizu: Ōe to murakami to nijūnen" [A literary map: Ōe and Murakami and twenty years]. *Asahi Sensho* 850. Tokyo: Asahi shinbun shuppan, 2008, 228–230.

Katō Norihiro. *Murakami Haruki no tanpen o eigo de yomu 1979–2011*. Tokyo: Kōdansha, 2011.

Kawasaki, Keiya. "Hinichijyō no tonneru wo kugurinukete: Murakami haruki to hanhenshyū sagyō" [Passing through the extraordinary tunnel: Murakami Haruki and process of anti-editing]. In *Murakami Haruki: A Journey into Movies*, edited by the Tsubouchi Memorial Theatre Museum, Waseda University, 155–160. Tokyo: The Tsubouchi Memorial Theatre Museum, Waseda University, 2022.

Kim, Choon-mie. "The Sense of Loss in Murakami's Works and Korea's 386 Generation." In *A Wild Haruki Chase: Reading Murakami around the World*. Translated by the Japan Foundation. Berkeley: Stone Bridge Press, 2008.

Kingston, Jeff. *Contemporary Japan: History, Politics, and Social Change since the 1980s*. Hoboken, New Jersey: Wiley-Blackwell, 2013.

Ko, Mika. "Adaptation as Cinematic Translation: Murakami Haruki and Ichikawa Jun's Tony Takitani." In *A Companion to Japanese Cinema*, edited by David Desser, 568–590. New Jersey: Wiley-Blackwell, 2022.

Lang, Jamie. "Pierre Földes' 'Blind Willow, Sleeping Woman' Will Get US Theatrical Run From Zeitgeist Films." *Cartoon Brew,* December 20, 2022. https://www.cartoonbrew.com/feature-film/pierre-foldes-blind-willow-us-theatrical-224301.html.

Lau, Jenny Kwak Wah. *Multiple Modernities: Cinemas and Popular Media in Transcultural East Asia*. Philadelphia: Temple University Press, 2002.

Lee, Chang-dong and Diva Veléz. "Interview: Lee Chang-dong at MoMA, Part 1 of 2—Burning Questions." *Screen Anarchy*, February 14, 2019. https://screenanarchy.com/2019/02/interview-lee-chang-dong-at-moma-part-1-of-2---burning-questions.html.

Li, Juan. "Murakami Haruki 'Pan'ya saishūgeki'-ron" [Murakami Haruki 'The Second Bakery Attack' studies]. *Ritsumeikan bungaku: The Journal of Cultural Sciences* 655, no. 1 (2018): 355–367.

Masato, Hase. "Murakami's Autobiographical Films as Subculture." In *Murakami Haruki: A Journey into Movies*, edited by the Tsubouchi Memorial Theatre Museum, Waseda University, 91–100. Tokyo: The Tsubouchi Memorial Theatre Museum, Waseda University, 2022.

McCormack, Gavan and Meredith Box. "Terror in Japan." *The Asia Pacific Journal: Japan Focus* 36, no. 1 (2004): 91–112. http://japanfocus.org/-meredith-box/1570.

Mori, Masaki. "A Bakery Attack Foiled Again." *Japanese Studies Review* 17 (2013): 29–50.

Mulvey, Laura. "Visual Pleasure and Narrative Cinema." *Screen* 16, no. 3 (1975): 6–18.

Murakami, Haruki, "Murakami haruki 2021 no miru" [Watching Murakami Haruki in 2021]. *Magazine House Brutus Tokubetsu henshū: Murakami Haruki* 12, no. 1 (2022): 118–123.

Murakami, Haruki. "Jibun jisshin no tame no eiga" [Films for me]. In *Murakami Haruki: Journey into Movies*, edited by the Tsubouchi Memorial Theatre Museum, Waseda University, 11–16. Tokyo: The Tsubouchi Memorial Theatre Museum, Waseda University, 2022.

*Murakami Haruki: Journey into Movies*, edited by the Tsubouchi Memorial Theatre Museum, Waseda University. Tokyo: The Tsubouchi Memorial Theatre Museum, Waseda University, 2022.

Murakami, Haruki. *Shokugyō to shite no shōsetsuka* [Novelist as a vocation]. Tokyo: Shinchō, 2015.

Murakami, Haruki. "Panya wo osō." Tokyo: Shinchōsha, 2013.

Murakami Haruki. "Drive My Car." Translated by Ted Goossen. In *Men without Women*. New York: Knopf, 2017.

Murakami Haruki. "Scheherazade." Translated by Ted Goossen. In *Men without Women*. New York: Knopf, 2017.

Murakami Haruki. "Kino." Translated by Philip Gabriel. In *Men without Women*. New York: Knopf, 2017.

Murakami, Haruki. *1Q84*. Translated by Jay Rubin and Philip Gabriel. New York: Vintage International, 2011.

Murakami, Haruki. "To Translate and to Be Translated." In *A Wild Haruki Chase: Reading Murakami around the World*, 27–30. Translated by Kay Yokota and Kawamoto Nozomi. Berkeley: Stone Bridge Press, 2008.

Murakami, Haruki. *After Dark*. Translated by Jay Rubin. London: Harvill Secker, 2007.

Murakami, Haruki. "Blind Willow, Sleeping Woman." In *Blind Willow, Sleeping Woman*, 3–17. Translated by Philip Gabriel. New York: Knopf, 2006.

Murakami, Haruki. "Birthday Girl." Translated by Jay Rubin. In *Blind Willow, Sleeping Woman*, 19–31. New York: Knopf, 2006.

Murakami, Haruki. "Dabchick." Translated by Jay Rubin. In *Blind Willow, Sleeping Woman*, 101–107. New York: Knopf, 2006.

Murakami, Haruki. "Tony Takitani." Translated by Jay Rubin. In *Blind Willow, Sleeping Woman*, 175–191. New York: Knopf, 2006.

Murakami, Haruki. *Sputnik Sweetheart*. Translated by Philip Gabriel. New York: Knopf Doubleday, 2002.

Murakami, Haruki. "Tony Takitani." *New Yorker*, April 15, 2002.

Murakami, Haruki. *Umibe no Kafuka*. Tokyo: Shinchōsha, 2002.

Murakami, Haruki. *Underground* [Andā-guruando]. New York: Vintage, 2001.

Murakami, Haruki. *Norwegian Wood*. Translated by Jay Rubin. London: Harvill, 2000.

Murakami, Haruki. *South of the Border, West of the Sun*. Translated by Philip Gabriel. New York: Vintage International, 2000.

Murakami, Haruki. *The Wind-Up Bird Chronicle*. Translated by Jay Rubin. New York: Vintage International, 2010.

Murakami Haruki and Shibata Motoyuki, *Hon'yaku yawa* [Night talks on translation]. Tokyo: Bungei Shunjū, 2000.

Murakami, Haruki. "Super-Frog Saves Tokyo." In *After the Quake*, 111–140. Translated by Jay Rubin. New York: Knopf, 2002.

Murakami, Haruki. "UFO in Kushiro." In *After the Quake*, 3–28. Translated by Jay Rubin. New York: Knopf, 2002.

Murakami, Haruki. "All God's Children Can Dance." In *After the Quake*, 55–82. Translated by Jay Rubin. New York: Knopf, 2002.

Murakami, Haruki. "On Seeing the 100% Perfect Girl One Beautiful April Morning." Translated by Jay Rubin. In *The Elephant Vanishes*. New York: Knopf, 1993.

Murakami, Haruki. "The Wind-Up Bird and Tuesday's Women." Translated by Jay Rubin. In *The Elephant Vanishes*, 3–49. New York: Knopf, 1993.

Murakami, Haruki. "Barn Burning." Translated by Jay Rubin. In *The Elephant Vanishes*, 131–156. New York: Knopf, 1993.

Murakami, Haruki. "Pan'ya shūgeki" [The bakery attack]. In *Murakami Haruki zensakuhin 1979–1989*, vol. 8, 31–36. Tokyo: Kōdansha, 1991.

Murakami, Haruki. "Pan'ya saishūgeki." *Pan'ya saishūgeki*, 7–31. Tokyo: Bungeishun, 1986.

Murakami, Haruki. *A Wild Sheep Chase*. Translated by Alfred Birnbaum. Tokyo: Kōdansha, 1989.

Murakami, Haruki. *Kaze no uta wo kike* [Hear the wind sing]. Tokyo: Kōdansha, 1979.

Nihei, Chikako. "The Productivity of a Space In-Between: Murakami Haruki as a Translator." *Japanese Studies* 36, no. 3 (2016): 383–397.

Numano, Mitsuyoshi, "Murakami - chēhofu - hamaguchi no mitsudomoe: "Doraibu Mai kā" no shōri keisai-shi. *Shinchō* 118, no. 10 (2021).

Ogata, Issey. "The Other Side of Happiness: Acting in Tony Takitani." In *A Wild Haruki Chase: Reading Murakami around the World*. Translated by the Japan Foundation. Berkeley: Stone Bridge Press, 2008.

Okamura, Minako. "Murakami haruki to hamaguchi ryūsuke to yatsume unagi: eiga 'Doraibu mai kā' ni okeru fukugoesei" [Murakami Haruki, Hamaguchi Ryūsuke, and Yatsume Unagi: Polyphony in "Drive My Car"]. In *Murakami Haruki: A Journey into Movies*, edited by the Tsubouchi Memorial Theatre Museum, Waseda University, 127–136. Tokyo: The Tsubouchi Memorial Theatre Museum, Waseda University, 2022.

Ozawa, Eimi, "'Watashi' ga kiete monogatari ga hajimaru" ['I' disappears, and the story begins]. In *Murakami Haruki: A Journey into Movies*, edited by the Tsubouchi Memorial Theatre Museum, Waseda University, 111–118. Tokyo: The Tsubouchi Memorial Theatre Museum, Waseda University, 2022.

"Pierre Földes on the Making of Blind Willow, Sleeping Woman." *Toon Boom*, June 28, 2002. https://www.toonboom.com/pierre-foldes-on-the-making-of-blind-willow-sleeping-woman.

Rubin, Jay. *Haruki Murakami and the Music of Words*. London: Harvill Press, 2002.

"Ryusuke Hamaguchi: The Multi-Award-Winning Director of *Drive My Car* on Adapting Haruki Murakami and Why Listening Is the Most Important Part of Acting." *Time*, March 28/April 4, 2022.

Strecher, Matthew. "Magical Realism and the Search for Identity in the Fiction of Murakami Haruki." *Journal of Japanese Studies* 25, no. 2 (1999): 263–298.

Strecher, Matthew. *The Forbidden Worlds of Haruki Murakami*. Minneapolis: University of Minnesota Press, 2014.

Suter, Rebecca. *The Japanization of Modernity: Murakami Haruki between Japan and the United States*. Cambridge: Harvard University Asia Center, 2008.

Suter, Rebecca. "The Artist as a Medium and the Artwork as Metaphor in Murakami Haruki's Fiction." *Japan Forum* 32, no. 3 (2020): 361–378.

Tamotsu, Aoki. "Murakami Haruki and Japan Today." In *Contemporary Japan and Popular Culture*, edited by John Whittier Treat, 265–274. Oxford: Routledge, 1996.

Tarkovsky, Andrei. "De la figure cinematographique." *Positif* 249 (December 1981).

Thornbury, Barbara. "History, Adaptation, Japan: Haruki Murakami's 'Tony Takitani' and Jun Ichikawa's *Tony Takitani*." *Journal of Adaptation in Film and Performance* 4, no. 2 (2011).

Tsui, Cynthia. "The Authenticity in 'Adaptation': A Theoretical Perspective from Translation Studies." In *Translation, Adaptation and Transformation*, edited by Laurence Raw, 54–60. London: Continuum, 2012.

Wakatsuki, Tomoki. *The Haruki Phenomenon and Everyday Cosmopolitanism*. Berlin: Springer, 2020.

Yamada, Marc. "Exposing the Private Origins of Public Stories: Narrative Perspective and the Appropriation of Selfhood in Murakami Haruki's Post-Aum Metafiction." *Japanese Language and Literature* 43, no. 1 (April 2009): 1–26.

Yamada, Marc. "Merging Matter and Memory in Cinematic Adaptations of Murakami Haruki's Fiction." *Journal of Japanese and Korean Cinema* 12, no. 1 (March 2020): 53–68.

Yamane, Yumie. "'Sekai bungaku' toshite no 'Bāningu': Murakami Haruki 'Naya wo yaku' wo Koete" ["Burning" as world literature: Going beyond "Barn Burning"]. *Hiroshima daigaku daigakuin bungaku kenkyū-ka ronshū*, no. 79 (2019).

Yomota, Inuhiko. "Murakami haruki to eiga" [Murakami Haruki and film]. *Sekai wa murakami haruki wo dō yomu ka*, edited by Motoyuki Shibata, Numano Mitsuyoshi, Fujii Shōzō, and Yomota Inuhiko, 137–152. Bungei Shunjū, 2006.

Yomota, Inuhiko. "How to View the 'Haruki Boom.'" In *A Wild Haruki Chase: Reading Murakami around the World*, 34–35. Translated by the Japan Foundation. Berkeley: Stone Bridge Press, 2008.

# Notes

## Chapter 1: The Cinematic Roots of Haruki World

[1] Tomoki Wakatsuki, *The Haruki Phenomenon and Everyday Cosmopolitanism* (Berlin: Springer, 2020), 77.

[2] Jiwoon Baik, "Murakami Haruki and the Historical Memory of East Asia," *Inter-Asia Cultural Studies* 11, no. 1 (2010): 64.

[3] Choon-mie Kim, "The Sense of Loss in Murakami's Works and Korea's 386 Generation," in *A Wild Haruki Chase: Reading Murakami around the World*, trans. the Japan Foundation (Berkeley: Stone Bridge Press, 2008), 66–67.

[4] Inuhiko Yomota, "How to View the 'Haruki Boom,'" in *A Wild Haruki Chase: Reading Murakami around the World*, trans. the Japan Foundation (Berkeley: Stone Bridge Press, 2008), 34–35.

[5] Wakatsuki, *Haruki Phenomenon*, 1, 4.

[6] Wakatsuki, *Haruki Phenomenon*, 46.

[7] Inuhiko Yomota, "Murakami haruki to eiga," in *Sekai wa murakami haruki wo dō yomu ka*, ed. Motoyuki Shibata, Numano Mitsuyoshi, Fujii Shōzō, and Yomota Inuhiko (Tokyo: Bungei Shunjū, 2006), 139.

[8] Aoki Tamotsu, "Murakami Haruki and Japan Today," in *Contemporary Japan and Popular Culture*, ed. John Whittier Treat (Oxford: Routledge, 1996), 268.

[9] Jay Rubin, *Haruki Murakami and the Music of Words* (London: Harvill Press, 2002), 2.

[10] Haruki Murakami, *Shokugyō to shite no shōsetsuka* (Tokyo: Shinchō, 2015), 103.

[11] Haruki Murakami, "Jibun jisshin no tame no eiga," in *Murakami Haruki: Journey into Movies*, ed. the Tsubouchi Memorial Theatre Museum, Waseda University (Tokyo: The Tsubouchi Memorial Theatre Museum, Waseda University, 2022), 12.

[12] *Murakami Haruki: Journey into Movies*, ed. the Tsubouchi Memorial Theatre Museum, Waseda University (Tokyo: The Tsubouchi Memorial Theatre Museum, Waseda University, 2022), 20–21.

[13] *Journey into Movies*, 3.

[14] Murakami, "Jibun jisshin no tame no eiga," 12.

15 Jay Rubin, *Haruki Murakami and the Music of Words* (London: Harvill Press, 2002), 21.

16 Murakami, "Jibun jisshin no tame no eiga," 13.

17 *Journey into Movies*, 26–27.

18 Rubin, *Haruki Murakami and the Music of Words*, 28.

19 For a complete list of films referenced in Murakami's works, see *Journey into Movies*, ix–xxvi.

20 For a complete list, see *Journey into Movies*, ix–xxvi.

21 Aaron Gerow, "Murakami Haruki ni okeru eiga to bungaku no kōryū," in *Murakami Haruki: Journey into Movies*, ed. the Tsubouchi Memorial Theatre Museum, Waseda University (Tokyo: The Tsubouchi Memorial Theatre Museum, Waseda University, 2022), 86.

22 Keiya Kawasaki, "Hinichijyō no tonneru wo kugurinukete: Murakami Haruki to hanhenshyū sagyō," in *Murakami Haruki: Journey into Movies*, ed. the Tsubouchi Memorial Theatre Museum, Waseda University (Tokyo: The Tsubouchi Memorial Theatre Museum, Waseda University, 2022), 156.

23 Eimi Ozawa, "'Watashi' ga kiete monogatari ga hajimaru," in *Murakami Haruki: A Journey into Movies*, edited by the Tsubouchi Memorial Theatre Museum, Waseda University (Tokyo: The Tsubouchi Memorial Theatre Museum, Waseda University, 2022), 114.

24 Matthew Strecher, "Magical Realism and the Search for Identity in the Fiction of Murakami Haruki," *Journal of Japanese Studies* 25, no. 2 (1999): 271.

25 Strecher, "Magical Realism," 271.

26 Issey Ogata, "The Other Side of Happiness: Acting in Tony Takitani," in *A Wild Haruki Chase: Reading Murakami around the World*, trans. the Japan Foundation (Berkeley: Stone Bridge Press, 2008), 101.

27 Rubin, *Haruki Murakami and the Music of Words*, 32.

28 Haruki Murakami, "On Seeing the 100% Perfect Girl One Beautiful April Morning," trans. Jay Rubin, in *The Elephant Vanishes* (New York: Knopf, 1993), 68.

29 Rubin, *Haruki Murakami and the Music of Words*, 250.

30 Murakami, *Shokugyō to shite no shōsetsuka*, 148.

31 Haruki Murakami, *Sputnik Sweetheart*, trans. Philip Gabriel (Tokyo: Kōdansha, 2001), 54.

32 Marc Yamada, "Exposing the Private Origins of Public Stories: Narrative Perspective and the Appropriation of Selfhood in Murakami Haruki's Post-Aum Metafiction," *Japanese Language and Literature* 43, no. 1 (April 2009): 1–26.

33 Laura Mulvey, "Visual Pleasure and Narrative Cinema," *Screen* 16, no. 3 (1975): 6–18.

34 Yamada, "Private Origins of Public Stories," 1–26.

35 Haruki Murakami, *1Q84*, trans. Jay Rubin and Philip Gabriel (New York: Vintage International, 2013), 13.

[36] Murakami, *Sputnik Sweetheart*, 123.

[37] Yamada, "Private Origins of Public Stories," 1–26.

[38] Haruki Murakami, *After Dark*, trans. Jay Rubin (London: Harvill Secker, 2007), 25.

[39] Linda Hutcheon, *A Theory of Adaptation* (Oxford: Routledge, 2012), 43.

[40] Murakami, *After Dark*, 26–27.

[41] Barbara Greene, "Alienation and *After Dark*," *Critique: Studies in Contemporary Fiction* 62, no. 1 (2020): 4.

[42] Murakami, *After Dark*, 27.

[43] Murakami, *After Dark*, 25.

[44] Barbara Greene, "Alienation and *After Dark*," 2.

[45] Murakami, *After Dark*, 134.

[46] Chikako Nihei, "The Productivity of a Space In-Between: Murakami Haruki as a Translator," *Japanese Studies* 36, no. 3 (2016): 390. Murakami is also somewhat reluctant to give authorization for adaptations. Fujiki Kosuke argues this reluctance is due, in part, to the poor quality of some of the early films based on his stories. See Kosuke Fujiki, "Adapting Ambiguity, Placing (In)visibility: Geopolitical and Sexual Tension in Lee Chang-dong's *Burning*," *Cinema Studies* 14 (2019): 73.

[47] Hutcheon, *A Theory of Adaptation*, 8.

[48] Hutcheon, *A Theory of Adaptation*, 20–21.

[49] Inuhiko, "Murakami haruki to eiga," 143–144. Hase Masato suggests Ōmori is one of the only directors Murakami entrusted with the adaptation of a complete novel because he wanted an amateur to adapt a novel that he wrote as an amateur. See Hase Masato, "Murakami's Autobiographical Films as Subculture," in *Murakami Haruki: A Journey into Movies*, ed. the Tsubouchi Memorial Theatre Museum, Waseda University (Tokyo: The Tsubouchi Memorial Theatre Museum, Waseda University, 2022), 92.

## Chapter 2: Crime on Camera: Screening "The Bakery Attack"

[1] According to Masaki Mori, Murakami borrowed the phrase "the gun shop attack" from newspaper headlines about the robbery of a gun store to create the title "The Second Bakery Attack." Norihiro Katō, "Bungaku chizu: Oe to murakami to nijūnen, *Asahi Sensho* 850 (Tokyo: Asahi shinbun shuppan, 2008), 228–230.

[2] Gavan McCormack and Meredith Box, "Terror in Japan," *The Asia Pacific Journal: Japan Focus* 36, no. 1 (2004): 91–112.

[3] Norihiro Katō, *Murakami Haruki no tanpen o eigo de yomu 1979–2011* (Tokyo: Kōdansha, 2011), 254.

[4] Gitte Marianne Hansen and Michael Tsang, "Politics in/of Transmediality in Murakami Haruki's Bakery Attack Stories," *Japan Forum* 32, no. 3 (2020): 411.

[5] Masaki Mori, "A Bakery Attack Foiled Again," *Japanese Studies Review* 17 (2013): 30.

[6] Mori, "Bakery Attack Foiled Again," 33.

[7] Mori, "Bakery Attack Foiled Again," 31.

[8] Haruki Murakami, *South of the Border, West of the Sun*, trans. Philip Gabriel (New York: Vintage International, 2000), 63.

[9] Masako Ishii-Kuntz, "Balancing Fatherhood and Work: Emergence of Diverse Masculinities in Japan," in *Men and Masculinities in Contemporary Japan: Dislocating the Salaryman Doxa*, ed. James E. Robinson and Nobue Suzuki (New York: Routledge Curzon, 2003), 200.

[10] Jeff Kingston, *Contemporary Japan: History, Politics, and Social Change since the 1980s* (Hoboken, New Jersey: Wiley-Blackwell, 2013), 60–61.

[11] Matthew Strecher, "Magical Realism and the Search for Identity in the Fiction of Murakami Haruki," *Journal of Japanese Studies* 25, no. 2 (1999): 267.

[12] Hase Masato, "Murakami's Autobiographical Films as Subculture," in *Murakami Haruki: Journey into Movies*, ed. the Tsubouchi Memorial Theatre Museum, Waseda University (Tokyo: The Tsubouchi Memorial Theatre Museum, Waseda University, 2022), 95.

[13] Katō, *Murakami Haruki no tanpen o eigo de yomu 1979–2011*, 289.

[14] Choon-mie Kim, "The Sense of Loss in Murakami's Works and Korea's 386 Generation," in *A Wild Haruki Chase: Reading Murakami around the World*, trans. the Japan Foundation (Berkeley: Stone Bridge Press, 2008), 66–67.

[15] Russ Fisher, "First Look: Kirsten Dunst in Carlos Cuarón's 'The Second Bakery Attack,'" *Slashfilm*, November 29, 2010, https://www.slashfilm.com/512433/kirsten-dunst-carlos-cuarns-the-bakery-attack/?utm_campaign=clip.

[16] Hansen and Tsang, "Politics in/of Transmediality," 420.

[17] Hansen and Tsang, "Politics in/of Transmediality," 422.

[18] Haruki Murakami, *Kaze no uta wo kike* (Tokyo: Kōdansha, 1979), 25.

[19] Haruki Murakami, *The Wind-Up Bird Chronicle*, trans. Jay Rubin (New York: Vintage International, 2010), 24.

[20] Juan Li, "Murakami haruki 'pan'ya saishūgeki'-ron keisai-shi," *Ritsumeikan Bungaku* 655 (2018): 356.

## Chapter 3: Unfaithful Adaptations in *Drive My Car*

[1] Haruki Murakami, "To Translate and to Be Translated," in *A Wild Haruki Chase: Reading Murakami around the World*, trans. Kay Yokota and Kawamoto Nozomi (Berkeley: Stone Bridge Press, 2008), 30.

[2] Chikako Nihei, "The Productivity of a Space In-Between: Murakami Haruki as a Translator," *Japanese Studies* 36, no. 3 (2016): 387.

[3] Mitsuyoshi Numano, "Murakami - chēhofu - hamaguchi no mitsudomoe: 'Doraibu Mai kā' no shōri keisai-shi," *Shinchō* 118, no. 10 (2021): 4.

[4] Carlos Aguilar, "He Made One of the Year's Most Acclaimed Movies. Ryûsuke Hamaguchi Talks about 'Drive My Car,'" *Los Angeles Times*, December 20, 2021,

https://www.latimes.com/entertainment-arts/movies/story/2021-12-20/drive-my-car-explained-ryusuke-hamaguchi-interview.

5 Aaron Gerow, "Murakami Haruki ni okeru eiga to bungaku no kōryū," in *Murakami Haruki: A Journey into Movies,* ed. the Tsubouchi Memorial Theatre Museum, Waseda University (Tokyo: The Tsubouchi Memorial Theatre Museum, Waseda University, 2022), 86–90.

6 "Ryusuke Hamaguchi: The Multi-Award-Winning Director of *Drive My Car* on Adapting Haruki Murakami and Why Listening Is the Most Important Part of Acting," *Time,* March 28/April 4, 2022.

7 Patrick Cattrysse, "Film (Adaptation) as Translation: Some Methodological Proposals," *Target* 4, no. 1 (2022): 53–70.

8 Cynthia Tsui, "The Authenticity in 'Adaptation': A Theoretical Perspective from Translation Studies." In *Translation, Adaptation, and Transformation,* edited by Laurence Raw (London: Continuum, 2012), 55.

9 Ryūsuke Hamaguchi and Łukasz Mańkowski, "On the Road with Hamaguchi Ryūsuke," *Sight and Sound,* November 16, 2021, https://www.bfi.org.uk/sight-and-sound/interviews/hamaguchi-ryusuke-drive-my-car.

10 Murakami, "To Translate," 29–30.

11 Keisuke Hayashi, "Murakami Haruki bungaku ni okeru sai hon'yaku o tsūjita sōsaku no hōhō," *The Nineteenth Princeton Japanese Pedagogy Forum: Proceedings; May 2012* (Princeton: Department of East Asian Studies, Princeton University, 2012), 30–39.

12 Nihei, "The Productivity of a Space In-Between," 389.

13 Haruki Murakami, "Murakami Haruki 2021 no miru," *Magazine House Brutus Tokubetsu henshū: Murakami Haruki* 12, no. 1 (2002): 118–119.

14 Aguilar, "Ryūsuke Hamaguchi."

15 Haruki Murakami, "Drive My Car," trans. Ted Goossen, in *Men without Women* (New York: Knopf, 2017), 14.

16 Haruki Murakami, *The Wind-Up Bird Chronicle,* trans. Jay Rubin (New York: Vintage International, 2010), 524–525.

17 Rebecca Suter, "The Artist as a Medium and the Artwork as Metaphor in Murakami Haruki's Fiction," *Japan Forum* 32, no. 3 (2020): 376.

18 Haruki Murakami, *Norwegian Wood,* trans. Jay Rubin (London: Harvill, 2000), 48.

19 Minako Okamura, "Murakami haruki to hamaguchi ryūsuke to yatsume unagi: eiga 'Doraibu mai kā' ni okeru fukugoesei," in *Murakami Haruki: Journey into Movies,* ed. the Tsubouchi Memorial Theatre Museum, Waseda University (Tokyo: The Tsubouchi Memorial Theatre Museum, Waseda University, 2022), 127.

20 Minako, "Murakami haruki," 127.

21 Aguilar, "Ryūsuke Hamaguchi."

[22] In similar fashion, the mediation of others helps Sachi, the owner of a piano bar, get to know her son better after his death in the story "Hanalei Bay," which was adapted into a film of the same name by Matsunaga Daishi in 2018. One day, Sachi receives a phone call that her son Takashi died from a shark attack in Hanalei Bay, Hawaii. He was surfing in the bay area when a shark attacked him. His foot was bitten completely off by the shark. Sachi heads to Hawaii to take care of his funeral arrangements and returns annually on her son's death anniversary date. She spends time there reading or looking out into the ocean, getting to know her son better through her relationship with two young surfers who befriended Takashi before his death.

## Chapter 4: Merging Matter and Memory in *Norwegian Wood*, *Tony Takitani*, and *Burning*

[1] This chapter is based on Marc Yamada's article "Merging Matter and Memory in Cinematic Adaptations of Murakami Haruki's Fiction," *Journal of Japanese and Korean Cinema* 12, no. 1 (March 2020): 53–68. It is revised and reproduced here with permission.

[2] Nathan Clerici, "History, 'Subcultural Imagination,' and the Enduring Appeal of Murakami Haruki," *The Journal of Japanese Studies* 42, no. 2 (Summer 2016): 247–278.

[3] Jiwoon Baik, "Murakami Haruki and the Historical Memory of East Asia," *Inter-Asia Cultural Studies* 11, no. 1 (2010): 64–72.

[4] Andrei Tarkovsky, "De la figure cinematographique," *Positif* 249 (December 1981): 41.

[5] Henri Bergson, *Matter and Memory*, trans. Nancy Margret Paul and W. Scott Palmer (New York: Macmillan, 1913), 21.

[6] Eric Berlatsky, *The Real, the True, and the Told: Postmodern Historical Narrative and the Ethics of Representation* (Columbus: Ohio State University Press, 2011), 61.

[7] Berlatsky, *The Real, the True, and the Told*, 61.

[8] Gilles Deleuze, *Cinema 2: The Time-Image*, trans. Hugh Tomlinson and Robert Galeta (New York: Continuum Books, 1985), 35.

[9] Claire Colebrook, *Gilles Deleuze* (New York: Routledge, 2002), 33.

[10] Deleuze, *Cinema 2*, 68.

[11] Ronald Bogue, *Deleuze on Cinema* (New York: Routledge, 2003), 6.

[12] The incorporation of time crystals in the cinematic adaptations of Murakami's fiction is fitting given the fact that crystals are physically present in his novels as well. Crystals serve as a node connecting the two different worlds in *1Q84* that separate the protagonist Tengo from his childhood friend, Aomame. Through time crystals, Tengo sees a ten-year-old Aomame fast asleep: "Now the light of the air chrysalis itself was softly illuminating its interior, like light reflected from snow. He was able to see inside, however dimly. What Tengo found in there was a beautiful ten-year-old girl. She was sound asleep. She wore a simple white dress or nightgown free of decoration, her small hands folded on top of her flat chest. Tengo knew instantly who this was." Haruki Murakami, *1Q84*, trans. Jay Rubin and Philip Gabriel (New York: Vintage International, 2011), 584.

[13] Matthew Strecher, "Magical Realism and the Search for Identity in the Fiction of Murakami Haruki," *Journal of Japanese Studies* 25, no. 2 (1999): 73.

[14] Matthew Strecher, *The Forbidden Worlds of Haruki Murakami* (Minneapolis: University of Minnesota Press, 2014), 71.

[15] Haruki Murakami, *Norwegian Wood*, trans. Jay Rubin (London: Harvill, 2000), 3.

[16] Haruki Murakami, "Tony Takitani," in *Blind Willow, Sleeping Woman*, trans. Jay Rubin (New York: Knopf, 2006), 179.

[17] Murakami, "Tony Takitani," 189.

[18] Deleuze, *Cinema 2*, 69.

[19] Bogue, *Deleuze on Cinema*, 6.

[20] Deleuze, *Cinema 2*, 70.

[21] Deleuze, *Cinema 2*, 70.

[22] Linda Hutcheon, *A Theory of Adaptation* (Oxford: Routledge, 2012), 161.

[23] Though Murakami does not often see adaptations of his work, he praised *Burning*, suggesting it was better than the Academy Award winner that year, *Parasite*. See Haruki Murakami, "Murakami haruki 2021 no miru," *Magazine House Brutus Tokubetsu henshū: murakami haruki* 12, no. 1 (2022): 118.

[24] Yamane argues that *Burning* and the story on which it is based constitute an example of "world literature." See Yumie Yamane, "'Sekai bungaku' toshite no 'bāningu': murakami haruki 'naya wo yaku' wo koete" ["Burning" as World Literature: Going Beyond "Barn Burning"], *Hiroshima daigaku daigakuin bungaku kenkyū-ka ronshū* 79 (2019): 51.

[25] Jenny Lau, *Multiple Modernities: Cinemas and Popular Media in Transcultural East Asia* (Philadelphia: Temple University Press, 2002), 1.

[26] Lau, *Multiple Modernities*, 1.

[27] Kim, Choon-mie, "The Sense of Loss in Murakami's Works and Korea's 386 Generation," in *A Wild Haruki Chase: Reading Murakami around the World,* trans. the Japan Foundation (Berkeley: Stone Bridge Press, 2008), 66–67.

[28] Irene Hsu, "How *Burning* Captures the Toll of Extreme Inequality in Korea," *Atlantic*, November 15, 2018, https://www.theatlantic.com/entertainment/archive/2018/11/burning-movie-imagines-working-class-anxiety-south-korea-lee-chang-dong/575773/.

[29] Hsu, "How *Burning* Captures the Toll of Extreme Inequality."

[30] Kosuke Fujiki, "Adapting Ambiguity, Placing (In)visibility: Geopolitical and Sexual Tension in Lee Chang-dong's *Burning*," *Cinema Studies* 14 (2019): 75.

[31] Hsu, "How *Burning* Captures the Toll of Extreme Inequality."

[32] Fujiki, "Adapting Ambiguity," 75.

[33] Daniel Kasman, "Mysterious Elements: Lee Chang-dong Discusses *Burning*," *Mubi: Notebook Interview*, May 29, 2018, https://mubi.com/notebook/posts/mysterious-elements-lee-chang-dong-discusses-burning.

[34] Bogue, *Deleuze on Cinema*, 120.

[35] Chang-dong Lee and Diva Veléz, "Interview: Lee Chang-dong at MoMA, Part 1 of 2—Burning Questions," *Screen Anarchy*, February 14, 2019, 3.

[36] Bogue, *Deleuze on Cinema*, 121.

## Chapter 5: Animating Haruki World: *Blind Willow, Sleeping Woman*

[1] Haruki Murakami, *Underground: The Tokyo Gas Attack and the Japanese Psyche* (New York: Knopf Doubleday, 2001), 237.

[2] "Pierre Földes on the Making of Blind Willow, Sleeping Woman," *Toon Boom*, June 28, 2002, https://www.toonboom.com/pierre-foldes-on-the-making-of-blind-willow-sleeping-woman.

[3] Ben Croll, "Miyu Adapts Haruki Murakami Stories with Novel Animation Technique in 'Blind Willow, Sleeping Woman,'" *Variety*, June 19, 2021, https://variety.com/2021/film/global/annecy-miyu-productions-murakami-blind-willow-sleeping-woman-1235000603/.

[4] Jamie Lang, "Pierre Földes' 'Blind Willow, Sleeping Woman' Will Get US Theatrical Run From Zeitgeist Films," *Cartoon Brew*, December 20, 2022, https://www.cartoonbrew.com/feature-film/pierre-foldes-blind-willow-us-theatrical-224301.html.

[5] The description of the animation process is based on the interview in *Toon Boom*'s "Making of Blind Willow."

[6] "Making of Blind Willow."

[7] Abstracted forms of animation, moreover, play in the background of scenes illustrating stories told by the characters while underscoring the realness of the scene itself. At the end of section two, an excerpt from John Ford's *Fort Apache* (1948), in a simple animation style, plays in the background as characters discuss a quote from it.

[8] "Making of Blind Willow."